TAKE OFF

LIFE ▪ REAL ESTATE ▪ RELATIONSHIPS

NICK DAVIS

TAKE OFF

Copyright©2020. Nick Davis Inc. All Rights Reserved.

All rights reserved. No part of this work covered by the copyright herein may be reproduced or used in any form or by any means — graphic, electronic or mechanical, without the prior written permission of the publisher. Any request for photocopying, recording, taping, or information storage and retrieval systems of any part of this book shall be directed in writing to Mr. Nick Davis.

Extreme care has been taken to trace the ownership of copyright material contained in this book. The publisher will gladly receive any information that will enable them to rectify any reference or credit line in subsequent editions.

This publication contains the opinions and ideas of its author and is designed to provide useful advice in regard to the subject matter covered.

All trademarks are of their respective owners. Rather than put a trademark symbol after every occurrence of a trademarked name, we use names in an editorial fashion only, and to the benefit of the trademark owner, with no intention of infringement of the trademark. Where such designations appear in this book, they have been printed with initial caps.

ISBN: 978-1-7324701-3-2

Printed in Canada

DEDICATION

I want to dedicate this book to my, son Jackson, my family, and everyone who has supported me over the years with my ups and downs. I want anyone who is struggling to know there is light at the end of the tunnel! Never quit!

NICK DAVIS
Oakville, Ontario
Canada

CONTENTS

	DEDICATION	3
	INTRODUCTION	6
	THE RISING PHOENIX	8
1	THE CARPE DIEM PSYCHE	17
2	GUILT-TRIPPING YOURSELF INTO REALIZATION	39
3	MOURNING YOUR LOSSES	55
4	THE YOUNGEST FRANCHISE OWNER IN NORTH AMERICA...OR NOT	72
5	LICENSING YOUR LIFE UP A NOTCH	78
6	IT ALL SPIRALS DOWN TO EMOTIONAL VALUE	87
7	NEVER SAY NEVER	108
8	JUST THE BEGINNING	138
	ACKNOWLEDGEMENT	154
	ABOUT THE AUTHOR	155

INTRODUCTION

This book is about a young, licensed Canadian real estate broker and a mentoring coach who is relentlessly pursuing growth and success in the real estate industry. However, the journey leading towards this prime success-time in his life was a road full of hurdles and thorns.

This book addresses internal and external issues that the author dealt with growing up as an irrational, gullible, and living-in-the-moment youngster. It addresses issues that flipped his life upside-down from time to time, which prevented him from establishing and nurturing healthy relationships with the people who mattered to him. These issues momentarily harmed his reputation in the real estate industry, where he was a sales representative who would leave the best of the best envying his success. It was just a brief period of struggle until the author manifested his personality into the person that you will explore in this book.

The author wants people like him who struggle with life in an emotional and mental capacity to understand and accept that they are not alone in this; there are countless people out there fighting similar battles, and one of them is conversing with them through this book. This book serves as an empathetic medium of communication between those still finding a way to overcome the trauma of having strayed from their goals in life and being self-destructive. It will uplift those who have triumphed and made a life for themselves after learning from their obliteration.

Hence, the book has been based on the themes of love, relationship, and motivational factors, which, for the author, are his well-prospering real estate and currently growing coaching business. This factor, otherwise, could be any other business or passionate drive for his empathetic readers.

NICK DAVIS

THE RISING PHOENIX

Often in life, it takes a hard hit to force us to come to our senses and contemplate our decisions and actions taken so far. The hit can be physical harm that leaves us in pangs and overwhelmed with fear to disallow a cycle of similar mistakes again. Whereas emotional and mental harm can traumatize a majority of people. It is the losses that an emotional trauma incurs that makes us reassess past choices and the value of everything that those choices cost us.

"There is no success without failures and losses."
—John Maxwell

TAKE OFF

There is something about losses that baffles me. For a significant part of my life, it never made sense to me how most success stories emerging in front of me, whether from my generation or the former ones, were subject to lessons learned from losses. I was always the kind of person who would be awestruck, pondering how human lives revolutionize overnight. Until the revolution was intimate enough to give me a taste of success, it was inevitable for me to invest my belief in Maxwell's verdict.

Even though I may appear excessively optimistic, but I have evidential results to substantiate the enthusiasm with which I have penned down my success story. Serena Williams claims she grew from setbacks and not just her victories. In saying so, she affirms that God's way of teaching us to do better is to make us suffer losses. We are all carrying our crosses to be in Paradise now, aren't we? The bigger picture demands that we undergo a time of testing, I believe.

Here's where all the hope sinks in; nothing lost cannot be replaced with something better to make your losses count. Every loss is a lesson learned. Nonetheless, Kissinger set out some ground rules of not fearing the pressure life puts on you because the output is worth the pressure. For me, it was not just pressure but also a sense of wandering. I could see myself losing track of everything for which I set myself out. All the effort that I had invested in building a corporate future was close to being derailed.

The relationships that I harboured out of love and concern were on the verge of collapsing, and some invariably did. The bubble of the reputation I had earned and haloed around myself over years of hard work and dedication was just pop away from bursting. Even if for a brief period, I had unintentionally yet frantically dived into a wreck without any idea of tracing my way back out.

When I finally got some headspace to traverse the medullas of my head, I allowed myself the leverage to believe that not all or anything at all was destroyed as yet. There was damage or rather collateral damage in my relationships. Mending was still a practical possibility that I could bring about. It takes a leap of faith to step out of a dark headspace like the one I was in. Trusting the process comes later, and it eventually dwells within you once you have successfully let yourself skid across the dark cliff to the one where light awaits.

That little ray of hope across the tunnel for me was and is my coaching business. I cannot wholly express how enthusiastic and driven I feel about the motive, following, and growth that my coaching business has promised me. The motivation behind taking the coaching business up a notch is to touch the lives of my audiences and my attendees in a way similar, or at least close to, how this mentoring wave in my life has touched me. I have positioned myself on a platform from where I can easily communicate with the youth and adults traversing diverse landscapes across the globe, struggling with internal and external conflicts, hoping and desiring to overcome those struggles to be their true selves if not all successful.

From the most intimate viewpoint, I can put this together to make sense of the fact that all the downfalls I encountered and was nearly choked under, I used them as stepping stones toward my triumphant feats. The road to success is never an easy one. Tears, disappointments, regrets, crises, time lost and enemies gained, relationships built and broken, nasty emotional roller coaster rides, mumbling and stumbling; despite all those obstacles and temporary heartbreaks, there is still an intense scope of improvement and advancement. No matter at which point in life you feel like life has come to a halt, I hope this manuscript reaches you somehow. When nothing makes sense, I hope this does, and I am sure it will because all you need to know is that you are not in an unusual battle. You are not a solo contender. There have been many; there will be many. How you glorify your downfalls and turn them around into success stories is all but a matter of choice. Stay with me, and you will understand exactly what I intend to convey.

Addictions — can be plenty. Distractions — can be frequent. Detour — is a common aspect. Lack of Commitment — affects each one of us at least once in a lifetime. Obstructions — are essential for a high jump. Opinions — are crucial to constructive personality development. I understand someone else's opinions should not define you; however, if there were no opinions, there would never have been the scope of looking at anything with a distinct eye. The monotony of perceptions is bound to be an obstruction in itself. If you continue ignoring constructive criticism considering others to be poking their nose in your life when they shouldn't, you will never be able to come to terms with your innate shortcomings. I will never suggest to let all sorts of opinions influence your life. I also understand that being in a dark place somehow blacks out your distinctive capabilities, but then again, we have all the time to figure things out. The reins are in your hands, and you have the right to monitor your pace of growth or failure for that sake. When I say you make a decisive choice of growing, it is you in reality who controls how long you wish to stay in your claustrophobic past. Pay heed to all opinions; classify and analyze which ones need your time and effort to implement in your life.

Since I brought up opinions, you should also know that opinions fluctuate based on your circumstances. Whether you are killing it on the dance floor or breathing your last, the people around will always have something to say about you. When I was making high-end sales in the real estate business, my competitors and spectators began harbouring hatred and envy. When I went down with my corporate identity, their opinions of me were slightly twisted to be used against me and cause harm to my reputation. Their opinions can only matter if you let them influence your next move. When you listen to your instincts based on your understanding of what you are pursuing, there is no way in the world that any darn opinion will count.

There is a problem with our generation, which I have vividly observed in forthcoming generations as well, with an inherent root cause, I believe. We are adamant. I was adamant. Most of you reading this book would be so adamant even to accept right now that there is anything wrong with your ways or approach towards how you are handling your life. Simply identifying that your life is all over the place is an accomplishment and push towards success. I had to take ownership of my faults and admit to myself that I made mistakes — not once or twice but multiple times. Regardless, I needed to stand up to myself and the people I hurt during the process, the dreams I swayed away from. I had to be accountable and responsible to make amends. People can counsel and direct you, but no one ever demonstrates how to step out of the mess that you got in yourself in the first place. I will not outrightly declare that it is easy to give up on addictions. I will never make false claims that it is not impossible to sober down from something that has controlled your life for the longest time; it is certainly impossible. Aren't we all about doing the impossible? Weren't humans created with that intention? It was impossible to traverse our solar system and the Milky Way, and also other galaxies around ours. Nothing stopped humans from achieving the impossible, from defeating the undefeated, surviving the crises caused due to the Amazon fires and COVID-19, and from so many things we considered impossible. What makes you think you cannot eliminate that impossible label from your life and stand to represent something that no one else in your circle could aim for or imagine you aiming for?

There is an metaphor commonly associated with success followed by the struggle, which goes like, "rising from the ashes." Considering the chronology of events that have occurred and sketched the map of my life, I can better place myself parallel to the this metaphor. You all are the "rising phoenix" that I never imagined myself to manifest into, but that is exactly how we initiate the cycle of underestimation. We are so used to undermining our capabilities and potential that we tend to kill every possibility of letting our potential flow over the brim. When all hope is lost, and you seem to find the tiniest, dimmest ray of fire in yourself, which can ignite you and your surroundings, embrace that fire.

From drinking at an early age of sixteen to unexpectedly and unwillingly becoming a father at the age of twenty-four, I still chose to use alcohol as my coping mechanism. I was on the brink of developing what you can call self-loathing. I was extremely vulnerable as a person and awkwardly puzzled about my life. Unable to identify the triggering factors behind all the bad decisions I made, I continued to take refuge in hating myself for all the damage I brought upon myself. Until I finally matured and started taking ownership of my actions. It took me a while to let go of the demons that lurked around me, controlled my actions like no other — I actually mean, by playing with my mind and dumping me under the weight of wrong choices and actions. Well, to put it together, it was more like something was guiding me to do everything that would lead to my downfall and deconstruct what I had built on my own.

I had several blackouts before I realized what was happening with my real estate business. Eventually, you'll know where it all started too. All that matters to me is that if I could see my business crashing back then, while I am now soaring high with my revenue and recognition, then. I want you to believe that you can accomplish the same.

Bad chapters of your life mould you to be the best version of yourself, but if you choose to let them define you, you will be making a mistake. A mistake you will surely regret, and many of us already do. Regrets are worth living through if you can convince yourself to gear for a counterreaction towards that regret. I identified the bridges I burnt, the people I hurt, the finances and time that I likely lost, and also the damage I caused to myself. The realization has brought me here today; it can take you places tomorrow. I was once in your shoes, and I wish to see each one of you reading this book to be in my shoes in the near future. Even if you feel that your problems are grave enough to make you feel suicidal, think of how that one action of yours can give satisfaction to those competitors who envy you while traumatizing those who look up to you. No problem in life is worth quitting on. Under a circumstance where it is jeopardizing your mental health, and a solution seems difficult to strategize, you should seek an alternative to detach yourself from the root cause. Quitting was never an option, and it never can be. You cannot quit on yourself, no matter what happens. When you can contribute so much to the world, contribute half of it to yourself when struggling with life. Whatever the case, whatever the struggle, whatever the pain and stress, however influential the demons lurking around you are — you are not going to quit!

TAKE OFF

CHAPTER ONE

THE CARPE DIEM PSYCHE

I felt my heart pounding against my chest when I tried to recollect my senses and struggled to open my eyes. I felt a squirming sensation in my eyes as I tried to open them slowly. Soul-lifting dizziness prevented me from sitting straight up and gradually overpowered me with a sense of shame. I was nothing less of a mess, physically as well as emotionally. My clothes were covered with dust in various spots. At the same time, my mind was promptly bombarded with haunting flashbacks of my misconduct, my oddly careless personality that I had unknowingly embraced, and the bewildering realization of what exactly I was doing with my life in general and at that point, sitting in front of a place that was not even my own.

NICK DAVIS

It took me a long while of awakening and contemplation to realize that I woke up on the path that led towards my ex-girlfriend's home. Waking up to that realization put me through a moment that I can, without any hesitation, call the nightmare of a lifetime. It was a jarring sensation that I felt down my spine; I am sure that it can aptly describe what I felt. For a moment, I felt like I was some homeless creature wandering around aimlessly. The way I spell this out for you is precisely how I felt. Why wouldn't I feel the way I did? After all, I was aimless and lost. I was lost in the frequency of my thoughtlessness that I failed to realize there was life beyond the hazy craziness of my actions. In an eye-opening moment, I identified the resistance that I had been raising for myself and that it was high time to admit to the need for a change. We have all heard of that one occurrence or dialogue exchanged that flips life upside down; this was my life-changing moment.

You know a bit about my life as a whole, and you may have a rough idea of the kind of person you are talking to at this point. However, the more we think we know, the less we know about a person. I do not intend to say that anything stated above was a mesh of deception and that I will unveil a very different personality to you by the end of this. Nah! Nothing like that. I am no Oscar winner to take out into twisted imaginations and disappoint you for being misled. You know bits and pieces of my life from all that you previously read. We are all exclusively formulated, extensively built, and knit characters of God, so there is more to me than your eye can meet. Hopefully, you will not just feel like you are with me on the same page; in fact, each one of you might be able to put yourself in my shoes at some point in this book where my experiences resonate with you.

Before being anything of the sort that I painted above, I would like to give you a slightly different focal lens to look at me at a time earlier in my life. Imagine the life of a teenager who has unmatched business knowledge for his age, who possesses talent and potential in him. Yet, he continues to live his life like there's no tomorrow. I was close to that teenager. I was a young Nick Davis who wasted away his money and academic career on alcohol and fun because that appeared to be a priority during my adolescent age. We have all had that phase in our lives where we are so carefree that we do not wish to pay heed to how irresponsibly we are spending our parents' or our savings. Today's future generations have learned and are driven to invest in businesses like real estate and other entrepreneurial startups, stocks, and other options, which could eventually lead them to some substantial profit. Like I said earlier, I am the one who had a good amount of knowledge and intense passion for being this business-minded person.

NICK DAVIS

Let's trail back to the basics. As a young boy, I grew up in the lush and swarming suburbs of Oakville, which is a little outside of Toronto, Canada. Growing up, I had an immense fondness for playing hockey. Not just hockey per se, I played a lot of sports from a very young age. I vividly recall that I was eight years old when I set the benchmark for myself to always excel at hockey and never perform less than my potential and passion for the game by successfully making my mark in the triple-A hockey team, the Oakville Rangers. Being on that team is the highest level of rank elevation that one can get while playing hockey.

It is normally understood that a talent you possess or a hobby that you are exceptionally phenomenal at flows in naturally and easily without much effort or force. Unfortunately, and fortunately, it took an intense amount of energy and motivation to bring me to a point where I could commit to sports, only so that I eventually and unprecedently excelled at it. I kept myself engaged in various sporting activities to establish and secure my status as a reputable athlete representing the school at sports functions. For an interestingly extensive period through my high school years, I had a girlfriend. Although high school love stories do not prolong or manifest into anything more than dating, which was also my case. However, we managed to stick around for a longer time than usual, and that certainly makes me rethink the fact that I do, or at least I did, have the capacity to hold on to relationships if I wanted to.

Stepping into my adolescent years, I was not even close to accepting the idea that life was equipped with weapons to attack me. It does not matter if those weapons were not guns and stones to break my bones; the damage they did to me remains unmatched by even multiple knife stabs. I was not emotionally or mentally equipped with the strength to face all the battles that I was charged with.

I come from a typical middle-class family. My dad was employed at a steel business firm while my mother was an administrative accountant at a construction firm. I was a younger brother to two elder sisters, Cheryl and Diana. Cheryl is six years older and Diana four years older than me. There is a common notion that siblings usually have some traits or behavioural aspects in common, or they can be polar opposites, which is a rare scenario. For some reason, I always felt like I was a different personality compared to my sisters. I was nothing close to them. I never had their mentality, approach, or attitude towards life; hence, my progress also differed. Even though there is no point in comparing my progress in life to my sisters', it just appears to be an essential element in understanding how I went so off-track. I always had an overwhelming feeling of being the odd one out, of being the black sheep in my family.

NICK DAVIS

As a family, we grew up in a comfortable lifestyle, so I cannot assert that I had a difficult childhood. The town where I lived was auspiciously welcoming, and the neighbourhood I used to interact and play with was also closely knit; everybody knew each other and looked out for one another. I had a comfortable childhood, and with care and affection from my family, I evolved into a young high school guy.

I was a social freak in high school. I wouldn't say I liked attending classes, and I clearly took no interest in what the lecturers were imparting, but I wholly used to enjoy spending quality time with my school friends. Not engaging or interacting in class was a certain deception of me being an introverted personality; outside the classroom peripheries and in reality, I was a go-getter. My sister Diana was the student council president of her grade while we were in high school. Diana has always been true to the tenet of being an older sister; she is that sibling role model that everyone would expect her to be in a family, setting an example for her siblings to follow. She never chose to shy away from her responsibilities, both the expected and the invisible ones. I recall that when I entered grade nine, Diana drove me enough to convince me to run for the student council eventually. As mentioned earlier, I was the black sheep. I had no hopes of even fitting the criteria for selection.

TAKE OFF

To my surprise, I qualified as a successful candidate and also made my mark as one of the council members. I am sure that must have been a proud moment for my sister, who was already an ambitious and reputable student in school. As for me, I was on cloud nine. I felt on top of the world having hit a milestone that I never thought I had the potential for. Especially considering it was an achievement similar to one that my sister would otherwise stand successful for. I felt extremely vivacious and positive that day. It made sense as to what I was doing and the direction I was headed towards. I never thought I could stand by my sisters' examples and do anything remotely close to what they do. However, it is always the little things that add value and happiness to our lives, leading to an exhilarating experience worth remembering a few years down the lane. I would know because I do not feel the need to stress my nostalgic dimension to recollect this event. Whenever I place Diana in context, my memory is jogged to recall my feat.

Having a sense of direction in life and a path to tread gives confidence and contentment to human beings. It suddenly makes complete sense to me today. Most of us walk the Earth aimlessly. Now that I think of it, if Diana were to harbour similarly envious feelings against me, I wouldn't have been where I am today. I am thankful that I had her ambitious spirit to take inspiration from and constant encouragement that kept my spirit uplifted. She made me believe that I had the capacity to contribute more than I thought, not just to myself but to the people around me. Today, I think being in this place and contributing my experiences and takeaways with you is all part and parcel of her impact on my life. It was her support and my grooming that secured me a spot in the student council that year.

Hockey did not leave me right until high school. Being on the team entailed living a specific lifestyle with respect to team practices, training, and championships, and I fully dedicated myself to the sport. I honestly enjoyed having the company of the people around me. I love it to date. However, what I did not realize was that there was something unexpected and somewhat volcanic effervescing up to the surface. I was not aware that by the time I recognized the battle that it was alarming me about, the volcano would reach eruption to spread its lava.

Living the teenage dream, we tend to ignore the signs and red flags that life constantly puts in front of us. We take things extremely non-seriously until we are presented with a particular battle and placed in a do-or-die situation; that is when we grab the experience by its hand, let it impact us, and take the lessons as they come along for a better understanding of future circumstances and be geared with prompt response mechanisms.

TAKE OFF

*"Sometimes, you will never know the value of
a moment until it becomes a memory."*
—*Dr. Seuss*

Enjoying it while it lasts, and making your moment count is something I have come to believe is important. Certain moments are life-changing. I think that night at the high school dance was my make or break moment. As a careless teenager would, I decided to carpe diem. It was November evening, a month in advance of Christmas, when the council arranged our first high school dance.

A little fun killed nobody, right? I was all about that mentality in high school. Before the dance could commence, I chugged down a mickey of vodka, which was a substantially high amount to get me drunk and out of my senses. I was all about shaking things up in high school. I am sure you remember when I said I was a "social freak." Embracing that title meant I had to loosen things up at the dance that night. With sheer irresponsibleness, I took responsibility for stirring some fun into the dullness. As usual, it all felt right in my head because our minds are so numb at that age to decipher between our right and wrong actions. More than anything, everything we do has the most illogical justification to substantiate the wrong. While gulping the vodka down, I had complete confidence that I had complete control over myself. Little did

I know I was farther away from any sense of control, and in fact, my school life began slipping out of my hands with this irresponsible act of "fun," of which I kept no track.

I woke up to an awful day bombarded with hearsays and mixed information concerning me that had been reverberating throughout the school corridors and rooms. I was dumbstruck when I was shown a mirror by my classmates of what exactly I was like the night before. I could not believe or even try to digest that I was making out with a girl throughout the dance. I was already reeking of alcohol, and this rumour definitely added insult to my injury, or I would rather say to my injurious reputation. I was sulking in distress and rotting in shame, merely hearing the claims they were making about me.

More than anything, I was puzzled because I could barely remember if all that actually happened in reality. My first blackout under alcoholic trance — I was just fourteen. The reputation that I had established for myself being on the hockey team, the esteem and position I secured on the council; it all went down the drain when I least expected my downfall. Back then, I was not even close to being consciously aware of my addiction in any way; it just seemed to be a normal, tipsy episode in the life of a gullible teenager.

TAKE OFF

I was kicked off the council board, and I let Diana down; I shattered her expectations and took her trust and pride in me for granted. She was utterly upset and disappointed that day. Big sisters never let go of you, and there is no abandonment when it comes to them. Diana persistently tried to give me the right direction despite my flaws; she was like my guiding light. However, life had something else planned out for me, I assume. I was pulled out of the path that she intended to make me tread on; I was no longer walking in the footsteps of an exceptional sibling-figure role model. Instead, I was dragged and drudged into a path of my own where I encountered struggles that I was completely unaware and incapable of handling, or at least I had no clue at all how to tackle those struggles in the beginning. I was hardly fourteen yet glued and caught up in a web of troubles due to my vandalizing idiosyncrasies.

Detention — faced it. Suspension — lived through it. Rustication — suffered enough of it. You name it, and I have undergone that particular process of punishment. It seemed as though I had a magnetic force that only knew how to attract trouble. It was the fault in my acts, not in my stars — that is a given. My tolerance and frequency for drinking never decelerated at any cost. It was as though I was setting new benchmarks for myself. I ended up being a disappointing child who regularly put my parents through a tough time at school; they were never before held accountable or answerable for the consequences of my sisters' actions. More than ever, at this point in life, the overwhelming feeling of being a black sheep began feeding on me. I was submerged in this sulking attitude, and while I was already gasping for breath, the school decided to get tougher for me. I enrolled in math classes that summer and then another summer, and then every consecutive year, the process followed. I felt as though external chaos was making me feel out of place in school and at home. I was under constant pressure. But, in reality, I was just playing the blame game. I was running away from the root cause of the battles that were tantalizing me, but there's only so much I could run. Constantly pointing fingers at the external factors that surrounded me, I was finding easier ways of escaping my problems. On the inside, I was screaming my lungs out in sheer helplessness. Each passing day, my heart felt like it was tearing apart in waywardness. High school trauma is so suffocating — it pierces you and disperses your shards all over the place. I learned to deal with it in my own ways, blaming and escaping, until I finally decided to emerge from the immersion.

As soon as high school was over, I went up north to join a college in Barrie, Ontario — all that travelling, effort, and money only to find myself intoxicated through the majorityof it. I began hosting massive parties, which

TAKE OFF

meant unintentionally inviting more trouble for myself as a growing adult. I was so obsessed with drinking and partying; it felt like a party-animal-like spirit had possessed me, and alcoholic exorcisms are way more exhilarating compared to demonic ones, I believe. The obsession led me to initiate a night club business that had mentally, physically, and financially consumed the life out of me. I was a typical party guy who was inherently born with and grew to have an exponentially ambitious inclination towards entrepreneurship. The amalgamation of being a social butterfly, a party fanatic, and a corporate-minded person led me nearer and intricately into the night club venture; I hosted bigger parties and earned my ticket to the business. I indulged in heavy revelry and dedicated an increasing amount of time towards the night club business, which undoubtedly bagged me immense revenue. However, the more money I could earn, the more I could spend and mishandle instead of transacting. The prospect of early money strayed me from my academic career goals and encouraged me to persist the easy way without worrying about a future at all.

I am sure each one of you reading this is aware of the consequences of earning early money the easy way. You can call it a smart move on the part of children who learn to invest in stocks, shares, real estate, and small business ventures. However, it is not the smartest move. Investments are always risk-based. The value of your property or monetized assets are prone to fluctuation without any prior notice, while these are also vulnerable to complete loss. Investing in such ventures makes sense once you possess extensive knowledge on tackling the losses and not becoming too ambitious, which is a common factor behind major downfalls during teenage and adult years. There is a sense of brimming overconfidence, which prevents you from paying heed to the red flags on your way while you continue walking it with pride.

I, for one, did not finish college because I was so full of myself and content with my earnings and the kind of lifestyle that came with it; I felt it was pointless continuing my studies. The world was spinning on my fingertip. I was in control of my life; at least, I felt I was. I was ready to run this world. I had no clue that alcohol was slowly and gradually poisoning my life. It was depreciating the value of the good things in my life, including the company of a good friend, familial support, career orientation, and the direction to pursue my academic goals. Whether it was school, college, or my workplace, I found enthrallment and purpose at every step with alcohol around. Otherwise, I was numb and lost. In a way, I found alcohol as a means of escaping my real-life issues, and the only way I could tackle them was by being intoxicated and irrationally making decisions. My rationality and sobriety had abandoned me, or maybe, I willingly abandoned them.

I do not encourage young males and females who are still in college to skip their studies. Seeking a way to bag easy and big money ruins their chances of opening a pathway to future possibilities of something far more colossal than what appears to be facing them in the present. Each of us has the right and leverage to pursue our dreams and ambitions. It appears to be a strong propelling factor, as I have observed in the current and upcoming generations that they are willing to pursue their ambitions alongside their educational pursuit. There is a wider gap between "alongside" and "abandoning." However, I did not quite well understand the difference during my adulthood.

Here I am, speaking to you today so that you can prevent yourself and your children from making the same mistake. It is easier believing that a college degree does not define your credibility than actually proving it. The degree makes a difference, not just to your credentials but also to your grooming and exposure.

Lost in the delusion of partying and losing my mind with the cashing I was doing, I started throwing massive parties at a club called Zu Bar in Burlington, Ontario. Our club hosted some of the most high-profile parties in

Canada, with top-notch quality of drinks and attendees. The club opened its doors to thousands of people every single night. The number of people kept accelerating as days and months passed by. We were on a roll with our business. I mean, entrepreneurial tactics are one thing I excel at; I had to do this right while everything else in my life was going terribly wrong. We managed to attract celebrities and corporate guests to our night club, allowing me to seek beyond the personal relations that I had already built over the years and exponentially expand my network of resourceful contacts. The idea was to transcend my comfort zone and reach new skylines with my business and PR network. Things were good. Things were taking off!

I have always been the person who manifests and nurtures mutually beneficial relationships considering the corporate expanse. The crowds I catered to loved talking and drinking over business possibilities and agreements. I loved being amidst the vast crowd the club invited over every night because I am a good chatter. I am sure that shows, doesn't it? (pun intended). I have always had decent relationships at and outside of the home. I think it was only due to my addiction and derailment that I harmed certain relationships unknowingly. I would have never, otherwise, intentionally harmed my relationships built over the years. Regardless, they were corporate, friendly, or family associations.

TAKE OFF

During this phase in my life, a loud club full of noise and chaos, fun and laughs, dancing, and chilling would make me feel miserable about my life. Deep down in the depths of my soul, I was sure that I was on the wrong path, and I could do so much better with my life. I knew I had it in me to improve, but I did not want to acknowledge it. Don't we all do that? We repeatedly feel our subconscious giving us alarming signals of being in the wrong place, choosing the wrong degree, wrong career path, wrong partner, or the wrong direction in life. It is so stubborn on our part to continue being regressive and ignoring our instincts. I believe it is more or less because we are all used to stepping on the bandwagon — to fit somewhere we can't, and belong somewhere we are not supposed to. I gave a kick-start to my entrepreneurial ambition, but in the wrong direction. I was confident that things were taking off, but I was subconsciously questioning myself, knowing that something was off.

WERE THINGS TAKING OFF IN THE RIGHT DIRECTION?

When I say I am ambitious and always have been, I was not cluelessly ambitious. I knew spang what I wanted and how I wanted to go about achieving it. I am a man of vision, a unique one indeed. I had a drive and motivation within me, which was supposedly awaiting its time to swim out to the surface. I think I had it sinking somewhere deep within me. My first pat on the back with my hockey triumphs associated with Bantam AAA 1986 as a member of the Oakville Rangers Club. Oakville Rangers remains close to my heart to this date, and I never miss out on any updates, matches, or people. Sheer dedication and love towards a place and team gave me a sense of belonging and being. Following sports, my being was driven by small achievements such as making it to the council and establishing a business early, even if it was wrongly directed. Ambition emerged right there.

As I matured into a version of Nick Davis who graduated from high school and entered Georgian College to pursue post-secondary education, my unique vision continued to expand. I could finally set a practical, achievable goal for myself. Now, the goal was to establish the first Porsche dealership in Oakville, which is why I pursued a degree in Automotive Management. My goal was huge, but the plan towards making that goal possible was indefinite and erratic. Sometimes, I feel like the synonyms of *young* should be reiterated as erratic and irrational. Everything we think of during our youth, including our choices and plans, pan out differently from what we initially envisioned. Unless your parents planned things, then there is a possibility of being on track and of things falling in line with the vision. I hope, and I am sure most of you can resonate with me on this thought, that most of our visions

TAKE OFF

pan out differently due to the demons we are battling inside our heads. Under peer pressure or a social acceptance dilemma, teenagers usually give in to drugs and drinking. In the urge to run away from a person who triggers your demons, you run away from home and the people you love. In the desire to materialize your greed, you abandon the things and people you love. To fulfill your cravings for lust, you dismiss your emotional responsiveness to people and situations. It is all due to the demons that lurk around you; it is not entirely your fault. But denying that you have no control over everything or at least some aspects of your life is partly your fault.

Even though I could not finish college, I started my business when I returned to Oakville. Things levelled up at a rampant rate. My business escalated sooner than I expected, and things were pacing their way towards success. A luxurious life demands or rather entraps you to give in to the temptation of temporary intimacy and physical relationships. The normative culture serves as a mandate to make you a successful businessman and be involved in an affair or emotional attachment with someone. Tausha and I started dating soon after I moved out of college. Tausha is also the mother of my son. We are not together. We dated for nearly six months, which was not even close to an intimacy that I would identify as emotional because I never opened up about my emotional demons, familial bonds, ambitions, or desires. To our youthful surprise, there is always a tomorrow. A tomorrow that poses a question mark at us for the actions that we are responsible for. My tomorrow after that relationship dissolved and brought new dawn into my life. Like every new dawn introduces a new chapter, which can be either good or bad, my new dawn brought the news of our son to me. Tausha was pregnant with my child, and I was just entering my peak career years at the age of twenty-four. When fathers see or hear pregnancy results under normal circumstances, they are amazed, and they react like the best thing in their life happened to them. It is like an achievement in life unlocked.

On the contrary, I went like, "Fuck! I cannot have this kid at any cost. I am in my early twenties, and this is not my time to be a dad. I am not prepared for this. What did I get myself into?" I assume that it might never make my son happy to hear this, but the pregnancy news put me in a dark place. I felt dejected. Having a child of my own, while I was acting like a child myself, was adding fuel to the fire that I lit in my life. A child was undoubtedly the last thing on my mind. To cope with the situation standing in front of me like a reality check, I chose to take refuge in alcohol. There was only so much that I could do to cope up. In the end, I knew I had to set my ways straight because I had to prepare myself for the dad role.

TAKE OFF

When Tausha was in labour, I went to the hospital while I was slightly drunk. It is such an irony that she allowed me to cut his umbilical cord; this was the life-changing moment that I spoke of earlier. In one moment, I could see both flashbacks and visions of my future playing inside my head. All the bad that had already occurred in my life, and if there was any good to come, everything was running wild through my imagination. I expected things to take a better turn from here, and I hoped to evolve into a better person for my son, at least. The moment I cut his umbilical cord, I was filled with the hope of making life better for my newly born son.

I thought it was really kind of her to let me cherish that moment because she did not want much to do with me otherwise. It was the year 2011 when I was blessed with my son, Jackson. Jackson is nine now; nine years of my persistence towards improving every passing day has not failed to surprise me. These years have been the most challenging period of my life, but the challenges in life empower you; it did the same for me. Anything difficult and arduous to attain is always rewarding in the long-term. What comes easy does not last long anyway. I live by what Roosevelt accepts as true, and I hope what resonated with me can also resonate with you.

NICK DAVIS

"Nothing in the world is worth having or worth doing unless it means effort, pain, difficulty... I have never in my life envied a human being who led an easy life. I have envied a great many people who led difficult lives and led them well."

—*Theodore Roosevelt*

TAKE OFF

CHAPTER TWO

GUILT-TRIPPING YOURSELF INTO REALIZATION

Jackson's birth was awakening dawn for me; it was a hope for reincarnation, if not physically, then merely through mentally evolving into a different person. I was confident that there was something or maybe everything that I was doing wrong with my life, and I stopped. It felt like my life came to a halt, and I was frozen in time, but I had to consider re-evaluating my life.

I decided to take a second chance with life and start by fixing what went wrong in the first place. I had lost track of my studies, and I was clueless about my academic career after I had dropped out of college. I made up my mind to apply for a real estate license. However, I relentlessly failed to focus on my preparation for the exam. I was not even close to putting in the right amount of effort required of me to pass that test. I continued to invest myself and my time in drinking and partying; the bottom line was, my awakening was back in the dark. It was just a momentary urge that I felt to get my life back on track, putting me on a guilt trip. Otherwise, I was still unable to focus on my studies. No matter how many attempts I took at the real estate license provision courses, I failed at them continuously. It was hard for me to retain focus in those areas of my life, which in reality required all my time and attention, which included my relationships with my family and loved ones.

After a few months passed by, I felt like I had enjoyed my cup of drinking and partying and wasting my self away, up to the brim. The drinking habit did not completely vanish. It was gradually fading away and would not overwhelm my senses and my existence in a demonic manner as before. As my addiction began to simmer down a bit and I started embracing sobriety in the most trivial steps possible, I realized that I was essentially geared to appear for my license exam. Without much hustle and with a few months of dedicated hours of studying, I was able to pass the exam and obtain my real estate license. I was thrilled and so proud of myself in that one moment; I felt like the license feat was a pat on my back for at least trying, struggling, and achieving something that I put my head to. I was elated with the progress I made.

TAKE OFF

KICKSTART IN THE REAL ESTATE BUSINESS

On my very first day in my real estate career, I listed a house worth $2.5 million. It sold fairly quickly. The business soon started rolling in. Immediately after my first sale in the real estate business, I listed another for $3 million, and it rapidly picked up. It was like money elevating itself and my life at the same time. One of my first real-time cheques was signed and cashed at a worth of $78,000. Can you imagine what it felt to have lost relations and my precious academic and career-building time, being slightly less indulged in alcoholism for all those months, and then suddenly bagging a hefty treat to yourself worth thousands of dollars? Boom! It was all bound to go downhill with that one increment in my earnings.

As a Canadian, or I would say, even as an average human being, a sudden surplus of money in your account or life is a magnetic force to attract evil, for me anyway. There is a great degree of greed and lust inherently present in the human instinct, and it comes to life whenever triggering factors like money, power, and the opposite sex come in. People generally claim money is the root cause of all problems in life and the solution to most of our problems. I could say this is partially true. Sometimes, all the money in this world is not enough to resolve your addictions or depressive state. However, after being so patient and careful with expenses and yourself, everybody feels it right to take a break from the monotonous and dull life and to break free into the social chaos.

    Here is exactly what happened to me. Money flowed , and I slipped into all things destructive. I indulged myself in the silliest and most unnecessary activities, taking up extravagant expenses and ignoring the crucial parts associated with money. I had lost all sense of understanding the value of hard-earned money. Once again, money flowing in easy and quick was triggering the demons lurking inside my soul ever since adolescence. With no sense of respect for money and where it came from and where it had to go, I stopped prioritizing my taxes, which I knew would surely get me in trouble in the long-term. I was derailed once again, holding hands with alcohol to keep me sane through all that insanity taking over me. Everything was spiralling and collapsing in a world of my own. A world that I had created in the delusional state of alcoholism. My efforts towards the real estate business were commendable, and people in my circle recognize that to date, the amount of effort I invested in growing my reputation, my business, and my lifestyle in the business did not go unnoticed. However, with significant achievements in specific industries comes great loss as well.

    I vividly recall that I once sold three homes in a single day. I was already recognized as one of the top sales repre-

TAKE OFF

sentatives in my company. However, by the time I sold the third home that day, I was overwhelmingly intoxicated to the extent where I had no control over my senses. My client refused to let me drive, and I forcefully grabbed the keys from her hand. To date, I am unsure of the outcome of that drive and where I landed and who took me out, or how I managed to be where I was the next morning. All I can extract from that memory is that I woke up on the office floor with a severe headache whenever I did. I was not sure of the consequences of that hangover that was yet to be borne.

On a mentally chaotic Friday morning, my manager approached my office and commanded that I should clean the clutter I had created all over the space with scattered bottles in every corner of the room and all possible dumping spaces. She specifically used this statement to describe the state of my office, which was, "Clean this up!" By the likes and tone of that statement, I am sure you understand and can analyze the gravity of her agitation with my regressive behaviour throughout my tenure at that company. She walked out of the office on me, asserting in an angry tone, "I want you to meet with us Monday morning," she said.

As much as I wanted to believe that was just throwing a fit of rage at me and she would ignore that incident from

NICK DAVIS

Friday morning, I was shaken to my core on Monday morning upon reaching the conference room. The broker manager called a meeting with our company's CEO based in Toronto. They did not say things I did not already know, but I realized that I needed a reality check, which came through that meeting. They started by admiring the positive aspects of my contribution to the company and said that I was one of their top young sales representatives who was shooting sky-high then with sales in the real estate business. However, all that success with a lack of decorum was not going to get me far in that industry, and that was something I should have expected coming my way. I appreciate that the company did not sugarcoat anything and gave it off to me straight, saying, "We are not sure what to do with you, Mr. Davis. You are exceptionally good at what you do, but what are we to do with all your skills and tactics if we cannot have you sober and consciously aware while dealing with your clients? You are intoxicated at all times, and you are making a mess out of the office space and your life. It is high time you got your life together, or you will lose better business prospects in the near future."

The company spoke to me for my betterment. They were all fond of me as a person, and they genuinely appreciated the sales skills I possessed. If not entirely for their sole benefit, they cared for my well-being to a certain degree. They convinced me about attending a rehabilitation

TAKE OFF

program at a treatment center in Malibu, California, by the name of Promises. I realized that I was not up to any good with my life if my evaluation was coming down to a single statement: "We do not know what to do with you."

I certainly did not shape myself and my future to project uncertainty of my presence wherever I go, whether a party, someone's home, a family event, or professional space. People in my life were so uncertain of whether they wanted me around or not, which made me consider if I was serving them well or not. I wondered if I was adding value to their lives and ventures. With them questioning if I was exhibiting a positive aura at all or not, I did not feel myself to be in a position to deny the offer being made to me. I agreed to attend the rehabilitation program at Promises.

On the surface, I agreed to go. However, I was internally all over the place; I was emotionally broken upon hearing all that I did at the meeting. It put me in a bad place. I felt like I was in a hell-loop, going back and forth with my decisions and moves in life. I continued contemplating the decisions I made, the direction I took in life, and how it brought me to this point where my presence in a place was in question. I ruined everything during my teenage years due to an addictive habit, and in my peak years of growth in the real estate business industry, in my twenties, I was continuing to deteriorate the trajectory of my life.

Following the meeting on Monday morning, I was supposed to remain sober for another twenty-four hours to travel to California. Unfortunately, my ability to control my urge and desperation for alcohol was no more an ability I could hold accountability for. When the chauffeur sent from my company came to pick me up, he could pick a whiff of alcohol from my breath. Instead of driving me to the airport, he dragged me back home in the airport limousine. I was sure that the chauffeur would report about my behaviour, my state, and my indulgence in drinks. Before I could receive a termination letter from my company, I decided to send in my resignation. I quit on my dream job per se because I did not wish for my colleagues or people in my circle to find out about my firing and the reason associated with it. Despite my embarrassing approach towards everything being said and done about me, I upheld my ego and chose to quit without properly coming to terms with my faults.

Today, when I look back, I realize how important it is to come to terms with reality in a moment of sheer delusion. When we refuse to embrace our faulty reality, we continue to give in to our deceptive façade of life and self that we create to invest faith in. In failing to accept the wrong and fix it, we relentlessly accept it as right, and then the cycle continues as it did for me. I switched companies, and my self-destructive, extravagant, and thoughtless lifestyle set in once again.

> *"You're trying to escape from your difficulties, and there never is any escape from difficulties, never. They have to be faced and fought."*
> —Enid Blyton

It all began here — you remember that time when I woke up on the path leading to my ex-girlfriend's house? That was when I was on the verge of collapsing under the influence of alcohol. My drinking routine and intensity had extensively aggravated to an extent where I would momentarily black out; numb and unconscious at that moment was when I found myself wasted in front of her house and woke up to the realization that I needed to get my life together.

When I say awakening, for the first time in my life, an awakening realization did change things for the better. The day I woke up around the corner of my ex-girlfriend's house that very night, I went to attend a program. At the meeting organized by the program members, I encountered people like me. It felt like I was meeting people from another dimension who were replicas, but distinctively modified versions of me with their unique façades. I felt at home when I crossed paths with each one of those attending that meeting. They were people with similar problems, internal conflicts, and external complications as me; they understood me, they empathized with me, and for once, I felt like I was in the right place in my life.

Often, we feel like we are unable to fit into a specific community or familial space in our life. If you have ever felt that way, then there is no harm in feeling so; you just need to understand, you were right. You cannot always fit in a place where people cannot level with you. Sometimes, it becomes essential for us to step out of the confinement that we have been channelled to believe is our only safe and belonging space. There is a world of diversity and experiences open to you, and you have all the rights to step out, explore where you fit, find people who empathize and not sympathize with you, and if not stay, then at least learn to come to terms with your problems by being around them. It is part and parcel of life; it is a rite of passage to evolve into the person you are destined to be.

It took me two years to navigate between the rooms of that anonymous program. Two years of a constant struggle to detach myself from my negative traits and overcome the dark experiences of my past. However, I maintained six months of sobriety within those two years, and then I flushed all that time and effort down the drain. I was back at it; the usual, abusive drinking routine continued until a life-changing December. In the year 2017, when on a casual December evening, I resonated my resolution within my conscious and subconscious dimensions of the mind and soul to affirm that I was done with alcohol and my drinking habits. I knew I was done.

I obtained my real estate broker license, which is considered the highest and most reputable education in the real estate business and industry. I had worked hard studying that course, to earn it, and to regain my long-lost reputation in the industry. I wanted to regain the trust of my clientele that I had built growing in the real estate business and those companies that recognized and praised me as a young top sales representative. I finally earned the real estate broker license after I had sobered up for good.

"I wouldn't be where I am today if I didn't get sober."
—Nick Davis

Once I had stabilized my business preferences and my work goals, I was then in the right state of mind to make amends in fixing my relationships back at home. After ensuring sobriety, I made up my mind to work towards being a better father to Jackson. He was my priority in life then and is to date. I may have been unprepared for him at a certain point in life, which was practically rational for me to feel in my unstable and young twenties. However, I stopped putting myself on a guilt trip for that because I embraced Jackson since the day he was born, and from the moment I had extended my hand to cut his umbilical cord. I continued to provide him with the best possible care in terms of finances and material needs. Now was my time to emotionally and soulfully connect with him, be there for him as the father he could look up to in the future, and fill in the void.

Among the bridges I burnt during my intoxicated journey through the teens and twenties, I drove myself away from my always supportive pillars in life: Cheryl and Diana. I drove a wedge, literally and metaphorically, between my sisters and myself. My sisters stopped talking to me because of my attitude and habits as a drunkard; my addiction pushed them away from me.

My whole family did not want anything to do with me. They did not even want to accept me as their own. In some way, they had emotionally disowned me, but I was biologically still a part of them. However, with all their grievances towards me they knew and acknowledged that I was trying everything in my power at least after maintaining sobriety to remain sober and revive my broken relationships. They gradually began talking to me and letting me be a part of their families and lives, including me in family-oriented events and gatherings while they were always supportive of my struggle.

> *"If you want to find out who's a true friend, screw up or go through a challenging time... Then see who sticks around."*
> —*Karen Salmansohn*

For once in my life, I was happy and at peace knowing that the gap I had allowed to widen in the relationship between my sisters and me was narrowing. I could finally think of achieving a good relationship with them, given that I tried my best to do what they expected of me as a brother to them and father to my son, Jackson; they expected me to be the best version of my sober self.

Before I could start rebuilding the bridges I had burnt, by laying the foundation again, block by block, I was hopeful that I would be able to make it happen. Hence, at the end of it, I learned no matter how far-fetched your problems may be, no matter how intense your dilemmas are, you will find a motivational light to pave your way out of the chaos. You will get through it, whether with help or all on your own; it won't matter. Your success lies in making it out safely to your destined position in life.

NICK DAVIS

"Sometimes, you have to get knocked down lower than you've ever been to stand up taller than you ever were."
—*Nick Davis*

My business reached new heights during this span in my life; hence, I decided to call this masterpiece that you are reading and engaging with *Take Off*. I also learned that apologies are a strong asset that human beings can use to revert the wrongdoings in their lives, cheer someone up, and add value to life. There was a considerable amount of bridges that I burnt while revelling. However, I apologized for my actions and learned to keep moving forward for the of the ones I loved and for my own sake.

"The bridge you burn today may be the one you have to cross tomorrow."
—*Nick Davis*

We all are susceptible to at least one or maybe multiple bad chapters in our lives. I have had several bad chapters, and I had an almost bad chapter when I had lost my reputation and job both. However, where I am right now in life, I feel like the bad chapters have closed, and I have already flipped pages into a positive chapter of my life. I hope it continues to get even better from here on, as long as I can promise myself and my conscience to stay on these positive pages.

TAKE OFF

> *"Ever tried. Ever failed. No matter.*
> *Try again. Fail again. Fail better."*
> —Samuel Beckett

I only quit on my job once in my life because I held my ego high and did not want to come to terms with my inherent flaws. You are a witness to what that did to me. Escaping from your behavioural patterns is not the solution; facing them and fixing them certainly is. I feel I can impart from these lessons learned that no matter where you find yourself stuck and struggling, you should not quit under any circumstances, whether in a corporate position, a domestic one, or in your head.

> *"Winners never quit, and quitters never win."*
> —Vince Lombardi

> *"Don't quit. Never give up trying to build the world you can see, even if others can't see it. Listen to your drum and your drum only. It's the one that makes the sweetest sound."*
> —Simon Sinek

People always judge you and form opinions about you in both good and bad days and chapters of your life. When I was a victim of alcoholism, they formed opinions and rumours about me to ruin my reputation, claiming that I was a notorious addict; that was an extremely tough spot for me to be in. So much so that I was unsure if I could continue to thrive in the same town or if I should give a thought to shifting my business and residence to another town. However, they formed envious opinions of me because they could not stand my success and progress, growing into the business now. They did whatever they could to bring me down back then as well, and they continue to do it so today.

The entire cycle of burning bridges in my life was a short-term process. The long-term cycle requires each one of you and me reading this to keep fixing our bridges whenever we damage them, right then and there. Make amends where you need to, but more importantly, try not to go back to the same toxic cycle that first caused you to burn bridges.

> *"If the bridge to your past is burned behind you, then you have no choice but to travel the path into a successful future."*
> —*John Di Lemme*

TAKE OFF

CHAPTER THREE

MOURNING YOUR LOSSES

"Failure should be our teacher, not our undertaker. Failure is a delay, not defeat. It is a temporary detour, not a dead end. Failure is something we can avoid only by saying nothing, doing nothing, and being nothing."
—Denis Waitley

Today, I offer coaching services and advise people about recovering from failures and achieve success in business and life.

Why do you think I qualify to be a coach?
~Because you are experienced and have attained formal licenses to practice your services?
That's one good reason. What else?

~Because you have great mentors.
That's also right. What else?
~Because you are successful?
Yes, I am today.

OK. Let me tell you the biggest reason of all. I qualify:

BECAUSE I FAILED — MANY TIMES!

I suffered many losses — in business and relations.

I have been in your shoes. Thus, I know exactly how it feels to lose your assets, reputation, and relations.

When I reflect on all the wrong decisions in my life, I can now honestly say I'm happy that they happened. They helped me change my mindset on the self-pity and regrets I had for every loss. I took my losses and failures as lessons to move forward.

People have different definitions of failure; to me, the most common, easy definition is lack of success like most people, or I can say the word *unsuccessful* defines failure for me. To keep things simple, I can agree with that to most.

With lots of success and fun that I enjoyed over the years, I have lots of stories that proved me to be the jerk, and I simply couldn't get along with other important things and people. Indeed, I can tell you stories about the money I blew on stupid shit, and I thought I had all the fun.

I had the most fun trips in my past days. Once I rented a jet to go to Cabo. It is an amazing resort city on the southern tip of Mexico's Baja California peninsula. It is a paradise to indulge in beach activities and nightlife.

I fell in love with Cabo because the place didn't reject me like most of my relations did at that time. I got a villa there, and champagne kept flowing day and night. I got the most expensive sports cars. Indeed, I had tons of fun because it seemed to be sort of the purpose of life.

I realize now that the most important things to me weren't important to me then, as I was wrapped up in a completely different world.

Do you wonder why you, at times, feel like you can't achieve your goal despite putting in all the effort?

When you make a mistake, you think you are not smart enough, and it makes you want to abandon everything. How can you trust more in your ability to make things happen?

Over the years, I've found that when people stagnate, it is for two main reasons. One is that they don't have a simple, practical system, or strategy for action, that they can use to achieve their goals. Secondly, they are afraid of exposing themselves and failing, and of the criticism they might hear later.

The core point I am trying to convey here is that we can learn from failure more than we can learn from our success. Those two things erode your confidence. They block you until you are left without motivation, without taking action, without seeing where you are going, and finally, you are forced to quit.

WHY DO PEOPLE QUIT?

Every time you feel like you are failing, other people are reducing their trust in you. Thus, realistic people hope that being successful is not so difficult, and there are no challenges on their way. There are two things that make the difference between people who achieve their goals and those who do not, i.e., their belief system and their habit system.

For someone who never made $500 in a month, thinking that he could make $5,000 per month would not be realistic, right? Here, your belief system literally doesn't support you. It could be a fantasy — one that sounds impossible and a goal that is not realistic. However, for someone who is making $100,000 a month, this thought would not make sense... $5,000 in a month? Something impossible? This has to be a joke! For this person, earning that amount is not a problem; it is something super easy. You see, they are two completely different internal conversations and completely different goals.

You must have heard many times that "You learn from failure." The interesting thing is, given the options, your brain learns from success and failure. Of course, the brain does not learn the same things or in the same way.

Every time you fail, your brain is drained of dopamine, making it harder to focus and recognize what went wrong. You experience more frustration, doubt, and fear. Your motivation is also affected. Failures and losses make anyone end up being apathetic and unwilling to continue working for their dreams. We can focus our mind to success with micro-successes.

Neuroscience is making things easier and easier for us; micro-successes can tremendously propel you to achieve more at work and in life. They positively impact your brain and your emotional state, which signifies feeling more optimistic, more joy, more courageous, and more focused.

People like to imagine experts and celebrities achieving great things overnight. In reality, the most productive and successful people use a strategy that never fails: they develop the habit of achieving goals, and they do it with baby steps.

To set brilliant goals, you need to develop the ability to set goals and complete them. Program your brain to see yourself as someone who achieves your goals because doing so gives you momentum. I had clear, brilliant goals, but I was not taking any needed steps to complete my goals. Instead, I was busy "enjoying" my losses.

In the real estate sector in Ontario, Canada, it is mandatory that you do a few courses to get your license within two years after you have finished your education. I knew I could do those courses easily, so I waited until the last minute to do them. I was so busy selling tons of homes that doing those courses wasn't on my mind, and I was literally inviting trouble.

I really thought I could convince the college to make an exception for me. In the meantime, my broker manager at the time kept asking me, "Nick, did you do the courses?" "Did you sign up, Nick?" She reminded me to do those courses and said they would come up so quickly. I don't know what had gotten into me, and I turned a deaf ear to her warnings. Finally, they came up, and when I went to register for the last course, it was so backed up that I couldn't sell for a bit.

At that time, my drinking problem had gotten close to its worst. I blurred the concept of reality. I knew, as a young top sales rep for a luxury real estate brokerage, people were going to use this against me. However, I came across a strange truth: "No one fuckin' cares what you do." It was all in my mind because, you know, it is all about Nick Davis. Right? Nope!

In junior hockey, whenever we lost in big games, I'd be one of the few that was crying in the dressing room after the match. The most memorable one was the OHL Cup. We lost to the Toronto Red Wings, and I think I cried for days. I knew this was the last year of our Oakville Rangers 1986 team together, and we were all going our different ways. Now I look back and cherish those memories and have nothing but gratitude for the friendships and times with my teammates.

Someone ends up crying when siblings or people fight with each other, and I hear that very often today when someone decides to start a new initiative. Most things don't work; most ideas don't succeed; most startups last three years or less. If you are the one behind it, the guy who always takes on things that fail, you are kind of labelled "doomed."

When we watch a baseball game or listen to a radio show or read a magazine article from a company that failed, it is easier for us to point the finger, identify a culprit, and criticize the things that did not work. It is like a social crusade to convince ourselves that avoiding failure is counterproductive. Here, I want to mention a few people who made their careers by often failing, such as Oprah Winfrey, Ray Kroc, Salomon Cohen, Paulo Coelho, Sylvester Stallone, Chris Gardner, among many others. Their failures were not due to mismanagement of something or a job poorly done due to a lack of interest. They are people with good intentions who want to do good things, succeed, and make a difference.

> "Failure is another stepping stone to greatness."
> —*Oprah Winfrey*

There are so many people who are paralyzed in the face of uncertainty at the idea of undertaking a project that one might come to think that we are programmed to be afraid. Scientists pinpoint where the reptilian brain is located; it is our prehistoric brain, the same brain that lizards have, full of fear and with reproduction as the main objective. The reptilian brain has been christened "resistance." Resistance encourages you to give in and avoid risky moves. In most cases, resistance always gets its way, sabotages our best opportunities, and spoils our chance of breaking the mould. Knowing can help you ignore it and develop your growth mindset with the acceptance of your reality.

When I look at all reasons for my losses and failures, I know most of it was my own fault. Unluckily, it took me a long time to realize it. Realizing my faults was the greatest thing that happened to me. Thus, that's absolutely OK. Overall, I look at all my failures and losses as lessons that no one else can teach me.

I believe that my failures have helped me beat the odds and grow further. One of the best pieces of advice I can give you is that you must learn from your failures and keep going, and you will grow for sure.

Another important thing is gratitude; it is one of the best qualities in life because it allows us to be in the present moment and enjoy every minute of our lives. However, what can you do during the moments that are not enjoyable but rather of suffering? Is it fair that we disconnect a bit? In moments of anguish, sadness, or failures, we can't disconnect ourselves from what is happening. All the moments we go through are necessary to mould ourselves into the person we want to be if we are willing for that to happen.

Sometimes, it is much easier for us to complain about problems that happen to us than to try to learn from them. There is also another group of people who try to focus on the objectivity of situations and don't allow themselves the time to feel the emotions they need to experience. When we repress our emotions, we hurt ourselves both physically and emotionally, and this is also not positive. Emotions are there to feel them, so it is okay that after a failure, you feel frustration, sadness, or even anger. What is not right is that you let those emotions take over you to the point of becoming your state of mind.

When you let yourself feel the hurt after a failure, your actions will be strongly marked by a predisposition to defeat. This type of behaviour won't work for you to recover, so the healthiest thing to do is to allow yourself to vent it out and drain all those emotions in a period that you consider sufficient, and then get ready to face your next challenge with enthusiasm.

Since we are emotional beings, having negative feelings is normal when something does not happen the way we planned. Above all, when we have invested time, effort, and energy, and it doesn't go well, the worst thing we can do to ourselves is to stop trying or resign ourselves after the loss. If you think it is not worth it and you have already decided to throw in the towel for good, you need to find reasons for why you should not let that experience lower your spirits and your desire to continue moving forward because failure does not define you; it is just one of the stages that we all must go through at some point in our lives. t would be ideal to achieve everything without experiencing downturns, but the truth is that without them, we would fail to obtain important lessons in different areas.

No matter how many times you fail, it does not define you; what defines you is the desire you have to keep going, getting up after each fall and returning to the ring with information and renewed courage to face the challenges from another rejuvenated perspective.

You also don't need to compare yourself to other people. Everyone has different processes that they must go through to achieve their goals. If you have coworkers who are always doing well and don't seem to have any kind of professional issue, you don't need to compare yourself to them. Instead, pay attention to know what they do that leads them to succeed.

The only person you should compare yourself to is yourself and if you consider that your "past self" had more successes, try to remember what you were doing at that time and what were the strategies that made you succeed. In addition, the success you had in your past can motivate you to achieve the things that you set out to do in the present and surpass yourself.

Sometimes, several attempts are required to succeed. If you get tired of trying after your first, second, or third failure, you won't be able to discover your true potential. This does not mean that you should get stuck in a single idea; you can change it, improve it, and renew it along with your strength. What you shouldn't change is your strong desire to succeed even if everything seems to be against you.

There are many known stories about all the times that today's great entrepreneurs had to try to achieve the success that they now have. Among them, we can name Milton Hershey (the creator of a popular chocolate brand), JK Rowling (the writer of the Harry Potter saga), and Steve Jobs. Apart from them, there are many more whose stories have not become as well-known, but that does not mean that they are less important or inspiring.

You must believe in yourself that you are capable of giving more, and it is another reason why you should not let failure make you resign and stop. There is much more within you; you just have to be willing to make an effort to bring it to light.

TAKE OFF

Maybe, the way you have done it so far has not been the right way, but that doesn't mean that's all you have got to give. You can always continue growing, challenging yourself to acquire new knowledge. It is a pity that you stop trying just because you don't think you are capable of moving forward after one or even multiple failures. One of the most important qualities to be successful in life is the quality of believing in yourself.

Mistakes are your learning opportunities, so don't waste them, and no one can take away these learning opportunities because these are the lessons learned through experience. You may be looking at the grey picture right now, but if you allow yourself the time to analyze what happened, you will notice the learnings, which will prevent you from tripping over the same stone again. Many times, failures are necessary so that you can take effective measures in situations that you will go through in the future. The healthiest thing is that instead of questioning yourself and feeling bad about yourself for the mistakes you make, it is to look for the learnings that you obtained during the experience; they will serve you in other circumstances as well. If you manage to understand the lessons, you will get practical learnings.

> *"Don't worry about failures, worry about the chances you miss when you don't even try."*
> —*Jack Canfield*

If we don't delve into the concept and meanings of loss and failure, we can hardly feel strong enough to tackle them when they occur. We can determine beforehand if we have tendencies that predispose us, placing behaviours that reinforce it within the scope of normality and actions that lead us to manage and minimize failures.

Most of us must have lived with great ambitions that translated into courageous and consistent efforts while failures invaded when we didn't yield the expected results. We make our balance, but possibly we are influenced under the same plans, moving in the same direction or in circles that connect us with similar feelings to finally give up.

Fear and insecurity find a comfortable habitat in failure. Internal conversations that silently and unconsciously feed messages to the detriment of the objectives and undermine their intentionality and perseverance in the person. Hence, the importance that it takes on when making turns or changes to ask ourselves two types of questions, i.e., reflective and restorative. The first I directed to a review or internal audit to establish possible causes based on our own propensities or weaknesses, and the second is to generate different actions covered by elements surely not considered and possibly will require external support to determine them and keep us on our path.

TAKE OFF

Ups and downs will always be present on our path to achievements, and fortunately, this is the case because they are the ones that provide us with sufficient skill in the different initiatives we decide to undertake. Both individually and organizationally, overcoming failures is linked to the vision and preparation that we have more than assuming positions of shielding against it, not the result of immediacy. It will have been generated by sometimes painful and disappointing learning processes, self-knowledge, honest criticism, and of course, a lot of work. As long as we are committed and willing to change plans as many times as necessary, correcting directions in favour of our objective, we will find the necessary potential because we will use our preparation by approaching it from a different perspective.

Today, we live in an extremely competitive society, constantly competing with our minds set on winning. We all want to win, that is clear, but that need to win leads us down a path that does not allow us to see and, of course, learn from the things that can happen on that road to success. That road to success is wonderful, and it is advisable to take advantage of everything that happens on it. Life comes with ups and downs, so enjoy both, or you enjoy half of your life. Balance is key.

I have learned that achievers and success-oriented people, including myself, use failure as a stepping stone to reach their destination. Usually, people don't like to talk in terms of failure because they don't like to lose; however, what is certain is that we have all failed at something at some point in our lives. The difference between those who achieve their goals and others is that the former knows how to capitalize on the teaching left by losses and failures.

Preparation is paramount in any training process and pursuing something important in your life, but realistically, no easy path leads to some attractive destination. In practice, obstacles, changes in plans, difficulties, and failures are the order of the day. By learning from failures, we allow ourselves to do a strategic self-analysis that allows us to recognize areas of opportunity to improve, the aspects that most affect our project, and something very important: "How not to do it."

Only the one who tries fails, only the one who wants to succeed in something tries, and only the one who is oriented towards success succeeds. To achieve success, dare to try, fail, and learn to get what you want.

I can assure you that doubts kill more dreams than failures; it is an open invitation to pursue something with enough passion and recognize the opportunities when you don't succeed.

You can regret, complain, and blame someone else or simply learn from what happened, recognize where you can do better, and make changes. The fundamental difference between a successful person and a failure is that both lose at some point, but the failure gives up very soon. Don't give up so soon; instead, go to your inner strength.

It is not always about winning; it is about learning and sharing what we learned, and I have written this book to share with you what I have learned. I believe it is important to win, but it is even more important to win when your victory helps others win.

To conclude, I would say that you can sit and wallow in self-pity about things that don't go your way, and trust me, I've fucking done it. Let me tell you honestly that there's nothing worse than self-pity. In my case I chanted "poor me, poor me" and it was ultimately translated into "pour me" and I developed a drinking problem. Every mistake I have made, and trust me, I have made a lot of them, but I now look back at them and take each and every mistake as a lesson that I can't learn anywhere.

"See failure as a road, instead of a wall." —*Scott Adams*

CHAPTER FOUR

THE YOUNGEST FRANCHISE OWNER IN NORTH AMERICA...OR NOT

One thing after another came crashing down on me, and things were falling apart. After some time, the Canada Revenue Agency (CRA) came knocking on my door. It turned out that they weren't happy with me, and it clearly meant more troubles. I took action and dealt with it. That wasn't fuckin' easy!

On the other hand, my relationships burned with pretty much every girl I dated and turned out most of their parents too.

At this point in my life, I felt like I hit rock bottom of my life and career. I was restless, and the only thing that could calm me down was a martini or straight vodka.

I was simply taking out my anger on myself and on other people; meanwhile, I was the actual problem. Unluckily, it took me a long time to accept the fact that I had a drinking problem. And luckily, I eventually realized that I was the problem.

Once I was sitting in a fine dining restaurant downtown Oakville by myself in the basement room. Of course, I was drinking an expensive bottle of merlot. I was on good terms with the restaurant owner because I'd dine in quite frequently down there. He, too, realized about my drinking problem. When he saw me on my own, he came down to talk to me. He said:

"Listen, son. You are going to be very successful. You have the personality that could sell anything. But, my God, you have to do something about your drinking. You are still young. Trust me. Try to get it under control."

At that moment, I laughed it off. But my drinking problem was so obvious that others could see it. And deep down inside, I also knew I had a problem, but I just wasn't willing to admit it.

Thus, I valued his opinion, and it crossed my mind: "Maybe, I should do something to try and calm down on the alcohol."

Of course, I didn't, at least for the time being.

As I thought over about my financial and social condition and my drinking problem, I realized what a mess I had become. That wasn't my destiny and destination. How could I stoop so low? I joined the real estate industry to break records and set new records. And I got such an opportunity to become the youngest franchise owner in North America with my old company.

When I was reaching a year of sobriety, I got a chance to work on a big business deal that would allow me to become the youngest franchise owner with the real estate company I used to be with.

I had thirteen agents on board while an investor offered me $3.5 million to open up a brokerage. That was a fortune I had been waiting for, so how could I afford to lose it? How could this happen early in my sobriety?

The deal involved big portfolios. I spent months with the vice president of Canada putting the deal together.

Everything was smoothly lined up, i.e., the location, agents, broker manager. The picture was almost complete, and the last piece of the puzzle was to get approval from the head office in New York City. I had done comprehen-

TAKE OFF

sive homework, and I was keeping my fingers crossed for the deal and hoping to be able to claim to be to be the youngest franchise owner in North America.

I applied for the franchise, and it didn't get approved.

We were in absolute shock. How was it possible when we were this thorough in our homework and preparation? No one on my team wanted to give up hope, so we stirred the plan up a little and applied again.

Of course, the deal didn't get approved AGAIN.

I had eight of the biggest owners in North America endorse me. So, what on earth were we doing wrong in that deal? We all became curious to find what went wrong both times.

As we investigated, we found out that the manager of the local office was not in our favour. In fact, she got a few more people on her side. She used my past issues against me and literally flew to New York in person to convince the head office that I would not be a good owner.

Did I feel like a failure because of that disapproval?

ABSOLUTELY, I DID!

NICK DAVIS

Had the old Nick been there, he would have done some serious damage to those who didn't favour the deal. Anger could have easily engulfed the old Nick, but he wasn't there. As I said earlier, it was the year of my sobriety. I had to stick close to those who helped me get sober, so I wouldn't fly off the wagon. I was in a dark, tough spot, wanting to drink.

What did I do instead?

Yes, I did the smart thing. I learned a lesson from that failure. It helped me accept it and move on. I didn't want to burn more bridges than I already had due to my reaction and anger towards people in the past. I took this event as a lesson and changed my ways of thinking. I put my sweat and blood into getting the brand out there, and it felt like a huge kick in the face.

A year later, I left the company. The same owners asked me to come back, but I respectfully declined their offer and wished them all the best.

The advice is simple: you need to learn from your failure and mistakes, no matter who was at fault. I believe this was the biggest test for me as a human being to grow from that event and change my ways.

TAKE OFF

I had the option to blame my failed deal on that local office manager and collect words of sympathy from others and grow a grudge and negativity inside. If I had done it, I would have multiplied the negative effects of that failed deal.

Not this time, I decided with firm conviction.

I took all this negativity and turned it into positive energy. Later, the vice president called me and said that I had such a good future ahead of me. He further added that he couldn't believe that I put that deal together as quickly as I did. Well, I get shit done; what can I say?

At the end of the day, the truth stared me in the eye that I hadn't become the youngest franchise owner in North America. However, the vice president was right that I had such a good future ahead of me. Maybe it wasn't the right time. That's life! Keep moving forward.

CHAPTER FIVE

LICENSING YOUR LIFE UP A NOTCH

The business of real estate thrives on mutual trust. Who could trust an undisciplined, addict realtor? I wouldn't. So, why would others trust me if I wanted to be in the business?

But I badly wanted to be in the business!

Why?

Because to me, real estate is more than just a business. It holds a special place in my heart and always will.

Since I have been through plenty of problems with my relations, I deeply understand the concept of a house made of bricks and a home developed with emotions and sentiments. Of course, real estate is my livelihood, but honestly speaking, I can never put a price tag on the pleasure and satisfaction I get when I help families find their homes.

I may sound emotional to many, but these are my real feelings. Through real estate, I am able to help others not only find a place to live but a place to build a home and a foundation. It is great to feel that you are part of building homes, not mere concrete houses. In homes, people grow their legacies and memories to last forever. As I said above, it is about making money, but the satisfaction and joy I receive knowing the fact that I am helping people to achieve their goals in finding homes provides value in my heart, and that simply is priceless.

Since the beginning of humanity, we have lived in society, which implies that the importance of helping each other to grow individually as well as collectively. Unity and empathy are essential traits, but today's competitive environment has put these traits at risk. As a result, our focus on individuals has also increased. However, I have learned my lesson the hard way, and I cherish this feeling of helping others.

Believe me, helping others makes perfect sense, and we need to feel it strongly. Helping others is the best medicine in times of crisis. When you help someone, your brain receives a feeling of reward, which generates a feeling of well-being and fulfillment. Knowing that you are capable of supporting another person, it makes you sure of yourself, and your social interaction also improves.

If you are generous to others, they will be generous to you. However, I may not say the same thing for your competitors. In fact, this is an interesting part where you can manage to have your competitors on your side. In real estate, there are many competitors, so your networking will matter a lot for your survival; well, this is another discussion. So, when others see that you give without expecting anything in return, they will want to show you their gratitude by being generous with you.

> *"Give, and it will be given to you. A good measure, pressed down, shaken together and running over, will be poured into your lap. For with the measure you use, it will be measured to you."*
> —*Luke 6:38*

By helping others, you help yourself. If you do good things for others, you will feel better about yourself and have the satisfaction of having helped them. There is more happiness in giving than in receiving.

TAKE OFF

Also, you must help yourself first. Helping yourself is an act of humility where you recognize that for any real change to manifest in your life, you must start with yourself first. Before trying to help others, you need to know yourself, identify your great potential, and, at the same time, accept your own fears in order to transcend them. When you are free from your limits, you become stronger and can clearly give true love and help to others.

When you focus on helping others without having made your personal change, you will be offering help of need and expectations; that help could not be called real help but an unconscious need to control and change others.

By the way, helping yourself first is not an act of selfishness but of wisdom. If you are free of attachments, you will be happy, and you can honestly help from your true self.

Starting with you first opens the door to your inner self who is always waiting to be heard to give guidance; when you go with it, everything becomes easier, the roads open, and you remember that in your true essence, you are a luminous being of pure love who deserves a life of abundant harmony and fullness.

Your inner self envelops you in your true identity as the master of love that you are and fills you with the strength and courage necessary to consume the voice of your false identity called the ego or fear mentality. That voice appears in your mind as thoughts of doubt, judgments, and condemnations that try to convince you that it is not possible to be at peace or live in happiness.

You are not your collection of past experiences that you call failures, but the false identity tries to convince you that it is. It feeds on the drama and personal stories that caused you pain, always trying to get you to fixate on the conflict. In this way, it weakens your personal security and your vital energy, consuming your potential to create and manifest true changes.

Your inner guide leads you to search within yourself for the path of freedom and fulfillment. The other guide is false and leads you to search outside through a labyrinth of limitation with no way out, where you project your imprisonment on others or on your affairs.

Helping yourself first is an act of love for everyone. By recognizing the love in yourself, you can really extend it to others. When you do not accept yourself from the heart, you will be unconsciously looking for love and recognition on the outside, hoping that this is the source of your happiness and personal security. Finding yourself lets you see that you can count on yourself, that your reality is that of a powerful being and that the strength you were looking for outside is always within you.

Letting go of the false image with the limiting past and with the drama will allow you to gain a whole world of possibilities, peace, and joy of being who you really are. When you sustain a life that does not fill you for fear that your world will fall apart, fear will control you. You will live a state of inner fear; for example, important people in your life will leave you; you will run out of money; you will not find the perfect partner, or you will make a fool out of yourself and fail if you dedicate yourself to what you like.

Living in this way is not living, and you will continue to materialize a false and empty reality because you are not vibrating with who you really are. This way, you will attract fake friends or partners, people who do not love you for who you are but for what you appear or represent to them, and an environment that does not support you but pigeonholes you.

You really get poorer every time you repress your mind and the desires of your heart. It is your choice to get out of whatever little box you have locked yourself in. You are a luminous and wonderful being, and only you can free yourself from all the impositions that you have thrown on yourself.

If you surrender to your inner self, you open yourself to the means by which your old image is transformed as you enter a fabulous undoing of your previous character, and you can return to your true essence. So, today help yourself first and let your inner fire consume your fears, let the wind take away the ashes, and your inner strength propels you back to life to resurface renewed like the phoenix that lets its old self die to be reborn.

You can learn to fly high and, at the same time, stand firm on the ground. Start following your heart. Follow your inner guide, reveal your luminous being, and allow your great inner power to sustain and support yourself and others unconditionally. Let me assure you that your true destiny is to shine. Remember that being you is easier than you can imagine.

I understand that the same failures that can set you back are going to develop the wisdom, insight, and empathy you need to thrive in the business world. I knew that the only thing stopping me from achieving success and applying what I had learned through trial and error would be the willpower and choice to follow through on my goals. Failures bring you the most valuable lessons that you cannot afford to waste. Thus, I had to ensure that my failures would not be squandered. Instead, I pondered on my setbacks and habits that caused the trouble I had been

TAKE OFF

going through and used them to my advantage, and readied myself to resurface once again.

Considering the mess I had been, success was the only option for me to come out on top again. The instruments I needed were my motivation and discipline. At the core of my motivation, different factors were driving me and inspiring me to move forward, no matter what state I was in. It did not matter anymore what trials, pain, and hardships I had encountered; I knew that I had to succeed for myself, for my son, and my other family members. Since I was at my worst, completely lost, broken, and hurt, it was then more than ever that I knew how important it was for me to conquer the challenges before me.

My past flashed through my mind, giving me a wake-up call. I had great academic records, and at one stage, I had to struggle to pass my real estate licensing exam. I had great relations, enviable success, and financial freedom. It seemed then all of it was gone in the blink of an eye.

They were all there a little a while ago; my beautiful son, my parents, my siblings, friends, and peers. I loved them, and I knew they were counting on me and believed in me. And the old Nick Davis was nowhere to be seen, and he was the one person I needed to prove to that I could and would conquer my demons, come what may!

There was a point where I knew that I was at a crossroads, and I could either give in and give up, hit the bottle again and watch my life plummet further and further into turmoil until my last breath, or I could turn my life over to the care of God and take action.

Again, it was hope in being a good father, son, brother, friend, community leader, and successful businessman that helped me to drive forward when all seemed to be lost. I love the real estate business, and I persisted with it to reclaim my former glory because of my natural ability and savvy people skills. I knew I could thrive, and the means by which I could thrive were my being a family man, community leader, and businessman alike. And my real motivation was my relationships that I wanted to make amends.

TAKE OFF

CHAPTER SIX

IT ALL SPIRALS DOWN TO EMOTIONAL VALUE

"When dealing with people, remember you are not dealing with creatures of logic, but creatures of emotion."

—Dale Carnegie

What a mess I was once! I wonder how I survived during that bad chapter of my life when all I did was to disappoint everyone near me. This included everyone, my parents, sisters, girlfriends, friends, colleagues, employers, clients, and even casual encounters.

My sister, Diana, who helped me at every step of my life, I even disappointed her. As a result, even my sisters distanced themselves from me, who were always there for me. I feel I was absolutely blank about the value of my relations. The only relations that existed for me were my business deals, parties, and alcohol. I lost sobriety and decency altogether. I was lying on office floors and streets fully intoxicated, which confirmed to me that I had developed an addiction, yet I continued with it.

Let me tell you that your family and other relations always matter, more than you think. At one point, I had developed great emotional distance from my own people who enabled me to live life and face the world bravely. No matter what they did for me, I lost them all.

I believe that holding on to emotional value in relationships and your loved ones are of prime importance. You can't afford to ignore them, and I am telling you this because I did so, and I faced the music. Even listening to the news of T's pregnancy did not make me happy. Instead, I became worried because my condition wasn't sober enough to nurture a child. I love my son too much, but I wasn't ready to have a baby at that time.

In 2017, I started realizing my condition, and I finally decided and mustered all my strength and willpower to get sober. Of course, I had to win my people back, and I started making efforts to revive my long-lost relations and mend the broken ties.

TAKE OFF

I knew that I had already damaged all my relationships and burnt bridges to get to their side on a positive note. There were so many contentions to dwell on, but talking about them would lead us nowhere. Hope has always been a saviour for me, and I had great hope. Thus, I decided to contact every person and let them know that I had changed for the better, and we all could start a new chapter.

Moving forward was the only option I could consider of. Living in the past does not do any good for anyone. So, I was determined to leave yesterday in the past and step into the future. However, I knew it would not be an easy path to tread on.

After hope, I needed bursts of courage to accept my faults with integrity, another instrument to succeed in relationships as well as business. If there is no integrity in our words and intentions, how could we expect others to even listen to us, not to speak of trust?

Thus, I was ready to make amends as I now had hope, courage, and integrity. There was once a good Nick, and he wanted to come back and take control to make things better. I made a promise to myself that I would prove myself to be a good man. I was sincerely apologetic, and I asked for forgiveness from everyone I had wronged during that ugly phase of my life.

When it comes to making amends with your family and other people, remember that empty promises will not work. Thus, I made a sincere effort, and I learned the true value of making a promise. My family members have such big hearts that they all welcomed me with open arms and forgave my past mistakes.

I could have been thinking, considering their negative reactions, and dropped the idea of reconciling with them.

What if they didn't listen to me at all? What if they insulted me for my past?

I could think of many "what if" scenarios.

In fact, there is no harm in thinking of the negative outcomes, but…you must not focus on negative thoughts. Instead, pay more attention to the positive aspects.

If you let negative thoughts pervade your mind, they can discourage you to even take the initiative; it blocks your way of communication, which is one of the core pillars of relationships.

Fill your mind with positive thoughts and attitude and stick to your words. This way, my positivity helped me garner trust and mend relationships I had tarnished.

TAKE OFF

Today, I have an infinite appreciation for my family, since they stood by me despite the toxic behaviour that repelled everybody. I can never thank them enough for their moral and emotional support. I had alcoholic addiction, and then I had the relapse phase, in which I could not keep my promises. However, I recovered from the relapse phase too, and all the credit goes to my family, my own people. I show my appreciation to my family by taking life one day at a time so that I can be the best person, always. Here, I learned one more thing that is about being there for others when they need my help.

How could I share with others if my own cup remains empty? Thus, I need to ensure that my cup is always full so that when others need help, I can respond positively. In fact, sharing is the key to having it all.

The act of sharing benefits the giver more than the recipient. Whether it is simply the act of listening or a shoulder to lean on, the recipient gets closeness to wholeness, inner satisfaction, and happiness. Sharing is an infinite force of all that is good, the strength we need, the love we long for, the response we seek, the inspiration we channel, the inner satisfaction and peace we desire. When we are connected to our inner being, we share more and also raise our consciousness.

In selfless giving, we can rise above our fears, pains, and problems. There is no limit to what sharing can do for us because it connects us to the source from where there is abundance, from where infinite blessings come, and where everything is covered.

When we understand that taking care of our people benefits ourselves more, we can begin to give more unconditionally, without needing anything in return, because deep down, we know that we are getting everything. The act of sharing and caring for others is about how to get it all and achieve happiness. The more you give, the more you receive. Thus, focus on sharing the light with your family and friends and carry this principle of sharing with others. Go ahead and share a little more every day, and you will feel much happier and more satisfied.

Since the year of my sobriety, I have been consolidating control of my life. Today, I am clearheaded and in control of my life enough that I can be there for others as the responsible and capable man I knew I always could be.

As I changed for the better, I got my family to share their love and kindness with me. Today, they see me in a new light and shower me with gifts of love, patience, and understanding. The support they gave me during the worst phase of my life helped me to be the man they can count on when they need someone reliable in their life.

I want you to believe the fact that you can beat all odds with the support and love of your family because they are unconditional. They understand you best among all the people around you. So, value them, and you will see wonders happening in every aspect of your life. The positive effects of your family's influence trickle down to everything you believe and do.

I am proud to say that my family is the backbone of who I am today. In our family tree, there are strong roots, and it means everything to stay rooted in our family values and emotional values. These family relations are our great teachers, and you can learn particular values from each and every family member. In the end, I gave up on addiction because I knew, deep down, that I could not quit on my family. Today, my source of inspiration and taking off is my family.

Every lesson I've learned through family values has shaped me to better grow and adapt as a leader in the family, business, and the community. The value of family and the lessons I have learned through them are indispensable for me to grow further. I know I cannot pay any price to learn these lessons of immense value.

NICK DAVIS

MY SON — HAS TAUGHT ME HOW TO LOVE AND APPRECIATE A CHILD'S INNOCENCE

In this maelstrom of feelings, responsibilities, things to do, career to get everywhere, and roller coasters of feelings that parenthood consists of, sometimes, I find myself standing, watching my kid; I just watch and enjoy to see him playing, sleeping, or watching a movie. There he is, and I can spend the whole day watching him. Children seem to be with no worries other than their own age. I truly think we have the best time of our lives in our childhood.

Innocence is the main fuel of children, their strong point as well as their Achilles' heel. There is nothing more wonderful than seeing how a child faces everything he sees. I think there is not a week without my son protesting and crying out to anyone who wants to stop and listen to him about how unfair a child's life is and how many rules he has to comply with.

For me, making children understand how lucky they are to be children and that they really are free is one of the most complicated things. This is how innocent they are.

Another great thing I learned from my child is sincerity. If you are looking for sincerity when faced with a question, ask a child and let them give their opinion freely. Today's children are no longer those little people without voice or vote or those who could not have an opinion. It is true that there is still much to do and that their leadership skills must be polished, but that will be given time. The important thing is that we sacrifice sincerity for the benefit of a good social relationship. The problem is that there are times when sincerity is necessary; otherwise, we run the risk of becoming falsified versions of ourselves.

The way they understand of friendship is something unique; it is a sort of intermittent friendship. One day they say that their best friend is so-and-so, and the next day they tell you that they are no longer friends and these names keep changing.

Their innocence and lack of prejudice make them see others as they are. In the case of adults, we have learned to hide our feelings, those that make us vulnerable or that expose our intentions to others, but a child does not; a child shows themselves as they are. A child only cares about how their friends are with them and the adventures they live together.

I believe that the future waiting for my son is tremendously exciting, and I hope I can accompany him in it for a long time.

NICK DAVIS

MY SISTERS — HAVE TAUGHT ME FORGIVENESS

I am forever indebted to my sisters for their forgiving attitude. When I entered grade nine, Diana encouraged me to run for the student council, and I successfully made my mark as one of the council members. Later, I messed it up big-time, and I was kicked off the council board. It was also disappointing for my sister, too; after all, she was my support and inspiration behind my running for the student council.

When I made a move to regain their trust, my sisters forgave all the wrong I had done. Their response taught me the importance of forgiveness in life. I realize that peace and further prosperity are not possible without forgiveness.

The action of forgiveness means forgetting the fault that another person has committed against you, and avoiding holding a grudge and thoughts of retaliating. We all make mistakes, and we hope we can be forgiven. If we want that, we must give it because life is a chain of reciprocities.

We are taught to say, "I forgive you," when we think we have been harmed. The reality is that forgiveness does not go there; the correct phrase is, "I forgive myself." Why? Starting from the concept of unity, where we are all one, and we must return to the creative source, if I am another you, then I am using you to harm me, to sabotage everything I want, and this is the most difficult learning to install in our consciousness since ego makes us tear down everything that threatens it. Having said that, we can see the importance of forgiving ourselves. Sometimes, we become innocent to the point of believing that we are perfect and that others are not, which is an egotistical act.

The ego makes you believe that you exist separate from everything. It is only your experience of separation that forces you to judge to keep the ego alive. Thus, forgiveness is towards yourself, with humility and acceptance, understanding that you use others from the unconscious to receive lessons. Forgiveness is an invitation to have deep introspection and look at ourselves with compassion.

An important step in learning to forgive is to be humble. The lack of forgiveness is related to pride, so the reason to forgive must be found in our deep conviction of not paying bad for bad. In addition to being an act of humility, forgiving oneself and others is an exercise of kindness and will allow you to place your trust in love for strength. Hence, forgiveness is an expression of love and is the basis of all healing in mind and body.

Learning to forgive means releasing the emotional backpack of all that is left over, that is, emptying the psychological burden of worries to give greater prominence to all the good that is about to come into your life. Learning to forgive means understanding that not everything in life is rosy. There are differences and hurts, and the best way to heal that pain is through forgiveness.

True forgiveness always invites you to free yourself from all ties of the past that prevent you from being happy today. When there is acceptance rather than judgment in your mind, the prospect of seeing life through conflict disappears. Anger, frustration, and regret turn into confidence and strength. Forgiving occurs as a response of self-observation and inner reconnection.

By looking inwards rather than outwards, the master of wisdom that lives within you is activated and shows you how to transform the way you view your past experiences. With its help, you can release judgments or ideas that tell you that your past experiences were wrong or shouldn't have happened.

If forgiveness has not occurred, consciously or unconsciously, there is a resistance to healing to let go or turn the page. In some part of your mind, you want to find a culprit that justifies why you cannot be free and happy in the present moment.

TAKE OFF

When you want to forgive without feeling it because you have been told that this is what you should do, and you do it because that is the "right thing to do," you do not free yourself, but you feel even more oppressed. True forgiveness cannot occur when you are motivated by fear or by control. These are not acts of courage but of guilt, which cannot have healing effects because they are not authentic.

Forgiving is a voluntary act of love, motivated simply by the desire to be free and happy. My sister forgave me because they always wanted their get little brother back. I can say that it was their choice, not a compulsion. I was the problem, and they turned out to be the solution. By deciding to forgive wholeheartedly, either to yourself or to others, you are inviting your inner master instantly to come to you, to assist you in your healing process from the past.

Today, decide to have an act of humility and ask your inner guide for help. Ask for it from your heart. Let go of your attachment to results and trust that help will simply come. By stopping doubting and opening yourself up to this response, you activate the healing. This is when people, events, and situations begin to come to you in sync to show you how to truly forgive. You then enter the miraculous flow of life, where the wonderful and different can happen.

Forgiveness happens when destructive beliefs from the past have been released. In this new state of mind, healing occurs naturally. You live in a free flow when you understand that your inner being has a divine plan for you and that each of your experiences is a necessary piece in the great work of your life. From this perspective, you can see the people and situations that come to you as the required teachers for your learning.

Forgiveness requires you to step outside the limits of your physical vision and develop your inner vision. Observing without judging allows you to release the expectations that you have formed about yourself or about others. When you are free of condemnations, you will be able to see clearly, and you will stop repeating past conflicts; you will turn the page towards new possibilities.

The most valuable help is within you and is always with you, but it is only you who can ask and take it. It is up to you to allow the limitless wisdom of your inner guide to envelop you in a state of peace and understanding.

Make the decision to forgive and open your mind to the happiness and freedom that you so deserve to experience. Forgiveness is your treasure! It is the gift that you give yourself and as an effect, also to others. The best time to forgive is always; here and now!

TAKE OFF

MY DAD — HAS TAUGHT ME DISCIPLINE

"Only the disciplined are truly free. The undisciplined are slaves to moods, appetites, and passions."
—*Stephen Covey*

Discipline — once, this word was all Greek to me. Nick and Discipline were literally entities poles apart from each other. All thanks to my dad for instilling and reviving the true meaning and practice of discipline in my life.

To start or complete a task, we need to have a certain mental and emotional state, and we assume that motivation is based on that. There is another way that does not mix the activity to be carried out with the mood and feelings, and that is discipline.

Trying to find a motivation to carry out a task bas become the most attractive food for procrastination. You often hear the expression, "I have not had enough motivation to do this." People wait to be motivated to carry out their tasks; meanwhile, we don't realize it, but we are conditioning our actions to feelings. What is forceful and important in all this is that if we are permanently waiting to be prepared and in the best mood, we may never start or finish something. Otherwise, we can see it in the discipline; by not subordinating the actions to the mood and feelings, discipline can help us achieve the necessary focus to get started as well as finish, within our allocated time frame.

Undoubtedly, there are multiple benefits that discipline brings. Discipline helps us do things that we want to do in a conscious way without stopping on how our feelings are regarding what we want to do; we can abandon the concept that we only have to do something when we are in the mood to do it.

I love the real estate business, and I am successful in this sector. I succeeded in the past, but things started to fall apart for me when I let go of discipline. Remember that discipline is the engine that once started continuously supplies energy to the system. And I turned off the engine on multiple occasions.

We may love doing some activity, but even there, we find elements that cause us displeasure, and that can lead to demotivation. Thus, the enthusiasm towards certain components of the activity that we love at that moment can decrease considerably. The mind says: "I do not feel like doing it." On the other hand, discipline executes the activity by making the decision to without invoking enthusiasm towards unattractive actions.

TAKE OFF

If we want to be efficient in a long-term activity, we must agree that it does not have adequate moods. The error lies in pretending to look at the execution of these tasks through motivation or lack of it. Consistency does not lie in being motivated; the answer lies in the discipline; it exceeds motivation in the attempt to achieve the appropriate state to start taking action. Hence, discipline arises when you must do something even if you are indisposed.

Our subconscious mind, which is where we operate from 95% of the time, works by habit. What you understand with your conscious mind will have no effect unless you begin by making even microscopic changes to your habits on a daily basis, without idealizing that you will get immediate results. It gradually creates a different structure that supports us in the execution of tasks.

I am eternally indebted and grateful for the love and support my family has shown me and done everything to regain control of my life and get back on track to success.

NICK DAVIS

MY MOM — HAS TAUGHT ME THE VALUE OF PATIENCE AND HOW AWESOME AND HOPEFUL LOVE TRULY IS

There is no love more unconditional than. No matter what they do, she always continues to love her children and leave no stone unturned to turn them into their best version. I regret that I could not be the best version of myself for some time, but she never abandoned me. To be honest, I cannot clothe my words to express my gratitude to my mother. However, I would try my best if my words can match what my mother really means to me. Here I would like to take this opportunity to express my feelings directly.

> "Mom, I owe you my life. If it were not for you, I might have been irreparably ruined to ashes. You are my strength, my blessing, and my source of inspiration to grow further. In my heart, your name will always be inscribed. Your sacrifice deserves all the prizes, and my purest loves will always be for you. You are my angel and always accompany me with great advice and love that remove sadness from my heart. You know all my flaws, my virtues, my worst and best moments, but you never cease to love me. You do it with no conditions, no judging, not expecting anything from me. I love you, and thank you, Mom, for your infinite love that I will never find anywhere else."

TAKE OFF

Let me tell you that you should not get tired of thanking your mom and expressing your feelings time and again.

So, the core values I learned from my mother are patience and the impact and shades of love.

"With love and patience, nothing is impossible."
—*Daisaku Ikeda*

Staying calm in the face of situations that have a negative impact on our daily routine is difficult. Patience is an art, a discipline that is practised, and a gift that is cultivated. It is not enough just to wish to be patient. It is perfected with time and experience.

Patience is the result of turning to the love and trust that resides within you. When you can let go of your attachment to results and worries about when you will reach your goals or when your wishes will come true, you begin to enjoy the moment you are in and allow your journey to become a process that is peaceful, harmonious, and even fun.

"To lose patience is to lose the battle."
—*Mahatma Gandhi*

By accepting that each situation in your life is occurring with a specific purpose, you are able to detach yourself from anxious thoughts, freeing yourself from the need to control people and events. Focusing on the present allows you to flow and find wonderful resolutions that you couldn't see before.

Patience arises when you follow the path that your inner guide shows you and not the environment that dictates you. Thus, you reconnect with the love that resides within you, which revitalizes and fills you with understanding. The more love you allow to flow into you, the greater the strength you experience. Opening up to love gives you the strength to go through seemingly endless moments or circumstances seen as unbearable.

> *"Patience attracts happiness; it brings near that which is far."*
> —*Swahili Proverb*

Patience comes from the creative source that resides within you. It is the source of unconditional love that teaches you to know how to wait and trust that your experiences will always give you the opportunity to evolve, even if at first glance they may not seem like it.

It is you who chooses to open communication with your inner being. When you do, your understanding of life rises, and the certainty that you are empowered to transcend every challenge that comes your way in your experience. Thus, you recognize that each situation is leading you to personal discovery and, ultimately, to the realization of your true and great self. The development of patience will be a reality to the extent that you allow your inner guide to show you the alternative solution to any situation.

> *"Patience is not the ability to wait, but the ability to keep a good attitude while waiting."*
> *—Unknown*

When you allow your mind to open and your disposition to settle, you will be able to attract the means required to overcome each obstacle that appears from this renewed state of mind.

> *"The key to everything is patience. You get the chicken by hatching the egg, not by smashing it."*
> *—Arnold H. Glasow*

CHAPTER SEVEN

NEVER SAY NEVER

A t one point in my life, I made a bad mess of myself, you remember? I was found lying intoxicated on the office floor. I believed that I had hit rock bottom, and I would never be able to give up on alcohol, and it made me abandon many of my relationships. When people are addicted, they tend to believe that they will never be able to give up on addiction. Thus, they fixate themselves on the belief that their life will continue to be a mess. I felt alone, and alcohol became my best friend. Like other people, I was also convinced that I had to continue my life with the mess I had made out of myself.

I said NO to my sobriety, relationships, and career. However, no matter how adverse circumstances are, you can never afford to say NO. Fortunately, I realized this fact, and unfortunately, it took me a great deal of time and many assets.

If you do a small survey of people close to you, asking what do you think of addicts? What are addictions for you? You will be amazed at the answers you will find. The most common answers will depict addicts as:

They are those people you see lying on a corner dirty and ragged. Yes, I was also found in this state on some occasions.

People who live on the streets and inject themselves.

They are people who do not have willpower, and they don't know how to control their life and relations.

Unfortunately, what these definitions reflect is apathy, stigma, prejudice, and a great ignorance about what addictions are and what the individuals are suffering from this terrible, chronic, progressive, irreversible, and fatal problem.

One of these examples we saw in the tragic life of the singer Amy Winehouse, who, like many others in silence and oblivion, suffered and was a victim of addiction.

NICK DAVIS

Addiction is a very complex disease that affects not only the individual but also all those close to them, and, you know, it is my firsthand experience. On this list of those affected, we can include parents, siblings, spouses, children, grandparents, uncles, friends, employers, clients, and coworkers. For each individual who suffers from an addiction, it is estimated that the number of those directly affected reaches eight people. In my case, it reached a much higher number.

Firstly, we must ask ourselves about the stigmas, apathy, and ignorance that we have around addictions. In simple terms, we can define addiction as the continuous use (conscious or unconscious) of some external stimulus (substance or activity) in search of a feeling of pleasure and escape. Using this definition, we can see that the range of substances and activities that fall within these parameters is immense — from alcohol to heroin, from investments in the stock market to video games, from food and shopping to relationships with others.

If we explore the reasons that lead us to remain ignorant, we may find that the subject generates some anxiety. If, to this, we add the social and cultural stigmas that surround addictions, we will find a phenomenon called denial. I was also denying my reality and considered my alcohol and mess everything. Exploring and learning about addictions can lead us to recognize in ourselves, or in a loved one, the reality of a present addiction. This reality can be very painful and lead us to a dilemma, i.e., confront it and face the pain and consequences, or protect ourselves, evade, and escape. Whatever the reaction, we must keep in mind that the addiction continues its fatal progression unless it is confronted and faced. For a certain time, I did not accept the fact that I had become an addict.

Those who struggle with addiction are individuals in great suffering, which could be conscious or unconscious. They are victims of a disease that gradually robs them of any measure of dignity, integrity, and values they possess. It turns them into strangers both to themselves and to other people, and it isolates and alienates them, leading them even to wish for and seek death as a way out of the hell in which they live. Of course, I did not wish for death, but I was turning out to be a social outcast from a social freak.

Informing yourself will give you the tools you need to firmly wage the battle against this subtle but deadly issue. If you think that you or someone close to you suffers from an addiction, remember that there are many experts and professionals willing to help you. Take action because your life or the life of someone you love is at stake. As for myself, I joined a program, and it felt much better when I found people like me.

People around addicts soon start giving up on them and make them sulk into this destructive mentality where they are only harmful to the people around them and can do no good to their loved ones or society.

In that meeting with the company's CEO and on the following trip in the limousine to the airport, ending up back at my home, I realized my situation, which led to my resignation. By the way, my resignation was another attempt to escape reality since I did not want other people to know the reason if the company fired me.

Remember that each case is different and therefore has its peculiarities. However, from the therapeutic statistics, it can be generalized that addictions are usually generated by very great pain that the person cannot bear and uses them to anesthetize themselves and thus not contact that deep wound. In this situation, self-esteem is the umbrella that can protect us from addictions or depressions, and our own worth begins to form within the family. Let's see it like this: "If a plant needs certain care to grow, i.e., water, light, and air, let's imagine how much more a person needs to whom thousands of feelings and values are transmitted in a changing and convulsed society."

What is more alarming as a parent is that your kids are exposed to a negative example, so the action of other family members is crucial, who can promote the healing of this parent, who with their actions show that something negative is happening in the family; something that quite possibly the other members prefer not to see. From this perspective, an addict can be seen as a scapegoat seeking to purify the guilt of their system through their own sacrifice. They allow the other family members the option to focus on their pathology rather than looking at themselves.

In these cases, the commitment of the family is vital, whose members must concentrate efforts to generate change and recovery from the unhealthy. It is remarkable that the addict is someone who already has a predisposition to addiction because not everyone who suffers a high degree of stress becomes an addict. For all this, it is essential to work on their structure, their drives, their behaviour, and their links. It is highly significant that there are competent bodies that devote their attention to all these cases and that work towards the better integration of each one of them in society. Support groups have shown their positive power to deal with these complicated dynamics, both for those directly involved and for their families.

I can't say that getting rid of an addiction is easy peasy, not at all. Here, you need some specific tools to fight off your addiction. At this point, faith, hope, will, and power are essential tools in your addiction recovery kit. Indeed, I used these tools to overcome whatever demons I had accompanying throughout the bad chapter in my life. It is your faith that brings you out of that delusional belief that people create for you; it is the realization of how they do not define you, and neither does an addiction define you, and it is this realization that brings you closer to accepting your reality.

You will often hear people saying when things are difficult, "You have to have faith." Even you must have advised others to "have faith" while you might have been struggling with your circumstances. But let me tell you honestly that it is faith and hope that brought me back on track.

Faith? It is simply belief, trust, or security and is generally linked to treligion; however, it can be applied in other areas of life as well, and of course, in business. Faith is synonymous with believing, so it is the fundamental basis to achieve things in our life. When we are confident that things can turn out to be the way we want, it makes them possible for us to do wonders, literally.

It is also important to live with faith in God; when you trust the Almighty, you feel courage, enthusiasm, optimism, and you are an energetic being, and times of uncertainty or changes don't scare you anymore. It is true faith in God that drives away fear and doubts since you

TAKE OFF

become willing to flow with full confidence. Although you do not know what will be ahead, you trust that God wants the best for you. If tests and challenges are presented to you, you also trust that God will never let you have tests that you cannot pass. Thus, with faith, you will always receive help from the heavens to overcome anything, and you will evolve.

> *He replied, "Because you have so little faith. Truly I tell you, if you have faith as small as a mustard seed, you can say to this mountain, 'Move from here to there,' and it will move. Nothing will be impossible for you."*
> *—Matthew 17:20*

Living with faith is extremely transcendental and makes a difference between having faith in God and in your abilities. To ask the heavens for something, you must do it with faith that your request is possible. Imagine that someone makes a wish to God, but in his heart, he doubts that it is impossible, will that wish come true? Just like you have in God, you have strong in your faith in yourself, too, and the mountains will move at your signal.

There are two important points that faith implies. The first is to be patient and know how to wait since God's time is not like ours. You want something with all your strength, and you trust that God will give it to you when the time is right for you. If you feel anxiety, it will generate doubts.

The second thing is that it is not only waiting for the miracle to happen; it requires that you take the step and go and make it happen. You can pray day and night, but if you stay static, comfortably trusting that it will come down from the above, maybe nothing will happen. The heavens are waiting for you to move, talk, search, work, and strive to support yourself so that the entire universe can be in your favour.

Faith is absolute trust, as it implies optimism, patience, and when the time comes, ACTION.

There are things that happen that are beyond our current understanding, so you must overcome them and trust. Everyone has suffered some sort of losses; however, faith and time have given them peace. I want to make it clear that it is normal that in some difficult moments of our lives, we can feel doubts; however, you must do not blame yourself for that.

Sometimes life gives us challenges that seem bigger than we think we can handle. In those cases, faith is a great ally because it helps us overcome challenges. When we face a challenge that we believe is greater than our strength, we may feel that the situation is at a disadvantage for us. However, I am certain that when we face it with faith and hope, we have a way to overcome it. Sometimes, I think God trusts us more than we trust ourselves.

The power of the human mind is unlimited, and more, if the impulse of the task to be undertaken comes from the heart and from what we believe is our truth. However, certainly not every time we have tried it, we have had the expected results. But this cannot be the excuse or reason for not trying again. Life will always give us challenges, and each of them, whether we achieve what we want or not, will leave us a benefit — a lesson. Sometimes, that gain, which is not what we had planned, over time, is even better than the one we originally wanted to receive. In both cases, I think it is about our faith, knowing that there is an infinite intelligence that guides our paths and delicately pulls strings in a perfect way. While I don't have all the answers, I have all the faith to continue.

At this point, I want you to believe that your reality is that you have the power to step out of the mess that you got yourself into the first place. Remember that no one else will ever be able to do it for you. It is your mess, and it is your responsibility. In your success toolkit, you have another great tool, namely your willpower, and it is not an illusion. I can assure you that it is a concrete asset of yours that you need to employ always.

Willpower emerges as a necessity when it comes to resisting the temptation or overcoming any challenges that life throws at you. I feel as if willpower were a magic formula or a protective shield. With it, it is possible to achieve everything that we can think of. And if we lack, well, we have to resign ourselves.

You can find people saying that it is just an illusion, a creation of the mind that depends on biological factors and the amount of sugar in the brain. So sweet of them, right? If we believe that we have willpower, we have a better chance of achieving what we want, even if that strength is more of an illusion than reality.

The most interesting thing is that this conviction is something that is learned and internalized. In experiments carried out by Walton and Dweck, they were able to verify that when faced with a difficult task, people who read sentences where willpower was valued ended up doing those tasks more successfully than those who thought of willpower as something limited.

People who think of willpower as an illusion often look for signs of fatigue, and as soon as they find them, they put tasks aside. On the contrary, when a person believes in his willpower and reaches the point of fatigue, he looks within himself for more resources to continue. It is your attitude towards a difficult situation or challenge that helps you explore your willpower.

"Nothing is impossible" is a classic cliché, but it is not an overstatement at all. I have experienced that it is 100% true. It is always possible to go into relapses, but in a similar way, it is also possible to one day resist the relapse and then deciding not to look back at all. I hope you remember how I went into the relapse phase. "Nothing is impossible" happened to me when I understood the essence of not giving up.

Without a doubt, one of the best-known cases of a man who faced an immutable truth was Galileo, who challenged the belief of his time that the Earth was the center of the solar system. He was forced to deny himself publicly on his knees. It is said that when he rose from this humiliation, he muttered under his breath the famous phrase, "And yet it moves."

In those days, the vision of the world espoused by the church was accepted by all mortals. In the twentieth century, science managed to take the place of absolute authority that religion had held, but not even physics, which advances on the basis of trial and error, was free of absolute truths. Starting from Galileo, Newton, and other giants of astronomy, it had been concluded that the cosmos was a precise clockwork mechanism where everything always happens in the same way. Likewise, it prevailed that time was an absolute thing that passed the same at any point in the universe and in any circumstance. With his theory of relativity, Einstein was responsible for dismantling that belief. In fact, he showed how as our speed increases, time would slow to a stop if we reached the speed of light, about 300,000 kilometres per second. And another absolute truth was born: nothing can travel faster than the speed of light. These concepts were thought to be impossible while they were already happening in our universe.

Thus, you will always hear people say, "It is impossible," or "You can"t make it," and things in a similar vein. No matter what, in the end, you will get to say, "And yet it moves."

> *"No one ever gets far unless he accomplishes the impossible at least once a day."*
> —Elbert Hubbard

You need to believe that there are no worse phrases than "Leave it like that" or "I can't do it" and similar

TAKE OFF

things with negativity and pessimism. These affirmations penetrate the depths of one's identity, becoming frustrated dreams. Turning, little by little, into a dark and frightening voice that continually tells us that it is impossible to do or achieve what we aspire to. Due to these situations, we find hundreds of people working unhappily on what they do not want because they were told that achieving dreams or doing what they wanted was not possible.

But it is never too late! There is always time to stop and go back to what we really wanted to do because there are no limits other than the ones we put on ourselves. For example, Jacob Barnett, a boy who was born with Asperger's syndrome, and his parents were convinced that it was impossible for him to learn to speak or tie his shoelaces. Not only did Jacob do it, but at the age of fourteen, he holds the title of the youngest astrophysicist in the world, among other achievements.

Another example is Pablo Pineda, who destroyed all myths by becoming the first person with Down syndrome to get a university degree in Europe and star in a movie. The list can be spread over multiple pages and books. The conclusion is the same: he, who wants can, nothing is impossible. It is necessary to repeat the idea that each person is the true absolute owner of their destiny.

NICK DAVIS

> *"Never give up on a dream. Just try to see the signs that take you to him."*
> —Paulo Coelho

Our limits are set by ourselves because the truth is that you decide who you should listen to and who you should follow and who we give power over our lives. And that is why dreams and aspirations must never be abandoned.

You can keep a personal diary in which you must write down the goals you want to achieve each day and what you must do to achieve them. Without forgetting what the possible obstacles will be and rereading it frequently, paying attention to what was recorded.

In the end, it is all about will and discipline, complaining less, and doing more. We do not have to worry so much about what is going to happen, but what we can do to change the situation. Thus, nothing is impossible, and the intensity of your wanting is your power.

I have developed a time-honoured, proven Five-Step System to achieve success in your business, relationships, and life. As you have finished reading and closed this book, you will actually close the book on failures, doubts, anxiety, and negativity in all of its forms. You will be able to start a new chapter in your life that will lead to your surefire success and growth. So, Nick Davis Coaching for success is based on the following five pillars that have also helped me build my business, my relations, and my life.

1. Honesty
2. Suit Up and Show Up
3. Communicate
4. Consistency
5. Stay Focused

Understanding these steps and values will help you learn the power of projecting yourself onto your desired outcome, and you will then materialize into that outcome. Remember that success and its positive impact drive you to be a better person every single day, especially when you have had the dishonour of seeing your worst that impacted your life and the people you love.

NICK DAVIS

HONESTY

> "Honesty is spiritual power. Dishonesty is a human weakness, which forfeits divine help."
> —*Mary Baker Eddy*

One of the qualities that we seek and demand of people is honesty, which is essential to encourage relationships to develop in a harmonious ambiance of mutual trust. The fact that honesty prevails in life brings something beneficial to others. The greatest honesty equates to a complete balance between what is thought, said, and done. It is not just about not telling lies, but it encompasses other qualities that anticipate a whole lifestyle. Reflecting on them implies putting order within each one and achieving transparency and integrity.

We can invent the most creative arguments to excuse ourselves, such as "Sorry," "I was wrong," "You're right," and so on. But we don't know how to be honest with ourselves or with those we say we love and respect. Could it be that we have forgotten how to be honest? Could it be that we no longer see honesty as an important value of the human being?

We live in a society in which most people have opinions on everything and judge everyone. It is as if being "cheeky" has become a value, covering up lies, deception, and humility. Honesty is a human quality, respect for the truth that we seek, and, in a certain way, we demand of the people with whom we share some type of relationship, whether they are friends, business partners, relatives, spouses, and children.

We must see honesty as an important value for human relationships to develop and grow in an environment of trust and harmony. It is a virtue that gives us security and credibility in people, and sometimes even admiration. Sadly, we receive messages that take us away from cultivating these types of values and bring us closer to a world of appearances and frivolity. Could it be that human beings have evolved that now security and trust are provided by other social appearances that are not related to honesty? And if not, why do we have it so backwards?

Human beings often tend not to want to face the truth of things because doing so implies taking action. At other times, we deny reality because we think that if we do so, at some point, it will disappear. But we soon discover that time passes and it does not; on the contrary, things get more complicated, accumulating one lie on top of the other, distancing ourselves more and more from that life of inner peace that we long to have.

Honesty leads to having the courage to ask ourselves the most difficult questions and answer them truthfully. These responses include our beliefs, duties, values, responsibilities, and attitudes towards life. If we long for a life of harmony and inner peace, it is necessary to be honest with ourselves in the first place.

A life without secrets, presenting ourselves as we are, knowing that the people around us love us and admire us for who we really are, not for what we project, it is a representation of the concept of honesty.

Know yourself, express yourself without fear, do not lose your truth, and fight for what you want. In any environment, it is everyone's responsibility to create a culture of honesty and transparency. More than complaining about the lack of honesty of others, the work begins with each one. Be honest because honesty is an antidote to evil, and it will be the armour that will protect you from what threatens your dignity.

TAKE OFF

SUIT UP AND SHOW UP

In life, we make decisions according to the needs, desires, difficulties, or goals that we want to achieve. We are often unaware of the failures we are making that affect our achievements in the short-term and long-term.

I entered into a strong awakening when I observed that my material and professional achievements were really limited compared to other people who had started in a similar situation to mine, and even with greater limitations, those people had taken their care very seriously. They showed consistency over the years, something I lacked.

To begin transforming my life, I went into a serious process of introspection and sat down to analyze a series of variables that were making the difference between others and me. After very careful observation, I then made the decision to be successful and turn my life around. And I found the idea of suiting up and showing up.

One of the great personal flaws that I detected was that I was dispersed in too many activities, and many of them were unproductive, and you know those activities very well now. I also tried to execute too many simultaneous projects. Thus, I was showing up in many places. Here, you need to curtail your involvement and stay focused, and set priorities. I have been through multiple challenges, but now I understand the importance of setting priorities and spending most of the time on a few goals to see great results.

Developing a new lifestyle of suiting up and showing up that leads us to the fulfillment of dreams tends to be difficult since there is a powerful inertia to return to the traditional model of behaviour. What I have discovered over the years is that most of our behaviour is unconscious, so that once we stick to productive habits, the new behaviour trend is created, and it becomes natural to be efficient, and we get used to it and get good results. It takes a lot of concentration and constant discipline to be able to break old mental patterns and adopt new ones to suit up and show up.

TAKE OFF

COMMUNICATION

When we refer to communication, we understand it as a common action that constitutes a basic process through which we coordinate and organize actions with others, and, therefore, a relevant process in any organization. When we focus on communication as a form of information transmission, we leave the human side of it and, therefore, all the richness and depth that we want to obtain is achieved. By the time we include the human dimension, we can realize the importance and significance of emotions in good communication. Given this, it would be of great importance that when someone tries to communicate and does not succeed, he is angry or resentful, for example.

Having fluent communication and, at the same time, projecting deep trust are essential attitudes to have an excellent organizational relationship to succeed. If a person or a company lacks communication, it can be said that it is destined for inefficiency and deep general discomfort, without any results and even very low productivity. Therefore, it is extremely important to develop these attitudes so that you can obtain better results and optimal productivity.

If you develop relationships of trust and communication in your work team, this will guarantee a more creative and highly cohesive work environment so that they can continue collaborating for the set goals and objectives.

If you work with quality in the communications that you maintain, this will determine the quality of your relationships. Now, it may be the case that you draw up a list of people with whom you may have bad relationships; then, you will observe and realize that they are going to be the same ones with whom you do not maintain good communication. In this sense, it is vital that communications with these people be improved, which would bring, depending on what was practiced, a solution so that the relationship can be much more effective.

Communication has to be seen as a kind of dance between speaking and listening, and in this dance, people with their own characteristics will participate, such as emotions, expectations, interests, knowledge, thoughts, among others, so that it will be fluid and well-orchestrated.

Teamwork, to be successful, must be based on tolerance. This must be cultivated by acts and maintained. Ensure that each individual in the group is able to maintain it and that the problems that arise do not affect the teamwork; through dialogue and communication, satisfactory agreements can be reached; also, confidence will be maintained and strengthened.

TAKE OFF

It should be clear that the greater the confidence, the greater the possibility of achieving the goals. In this sense, if you have little confidence, the possibility of achieving a goal is minimized. Therefore, confidence increases productivity, and the work environment becomes more pleasant and conducive to successful management and growth.

Effective communication also builds and improves trust. One of the primary characteristics of communication is being able to influence individuals and the possibility of enhancing and maintaining trust. In the case of losing trust, inconsistencies arise between what is said and what is done, or when the messages are perceived as unattainable promises or with manipulative overtones. Therefore, the relationship between communication and trust will depend on the efficiency of the former in the design of the strategies and messages and the veracity of these.

In relation to strategic communication, this is to be understood as that power to influence through communication on opinions, acts, and concrete facts.

CONSISTENCY

Consistency shows that you are stable and reliable. If you behave in a consistent way, others can expect the same kind of attitude and response from you when faced with different life situations that may emerge unexpectedly. Being consistent means that your character, attitude, and conduct remain constant for a long time.

Consistency is important since it is the foundation of trust. If you are able to maintain a consistent attitude, you can establish a productive relationship with others. There are times when it is necessary to give you some information that can be difficult, and when you are constant, others are more confident in giving you the news, anticipating more or less what your reaction will be. If you are unpredictable, everything changes, and relationships with others will become more volatile and difficult.

The people around you need to have someone to trust. If your boss, your business partner, or spouse sees that you are a person who works hard today and not tomorrow, they will not trust you or see you as someone interested in the relationship, which can be fatal for your romantic, work, and social relationships.

When two people are happy with each other, there is harmony, which is a vital foundation for a strong and stable relationship. The more consistent you are in your character, the less your partner will worry about the relationship and the fewer problems you will have overall. Consistency enables happiness, mutual trust, and helps improve your self-esteem.

Parents are the role models for their children. If you are consistent, you will set a good example for your little ones to follow. Remember that the pattern to be followed by children is the behaviour of their parents, and without consistency, you cannot demand obedience and respect.

Money is not the only thing in the world, but it is important for your relationship and your family, and this fact that can't be ignored. Being consistent is very helpful because it allows you to maintain a stable job or business and receive a constant income.

NICK DAVIS

STAY FOCUSED

Many people often feel determined and willing to do whatever it takes to get their business done. Feeling this way for a few days or weeks is not a rare sensation.

However, to truly be successful, you must be able to stay focused and inspired by what you are doing for months and years. It is a discipline that you must have yourself to see long-term success.

Being in business is not a short-term game; you have victories and losses, making it a matter of staying focused through all the ups and downs. You must be prepared to ride the roller coaster of excitement and disappointment as you develop your life, relations, and business. Accepting that this is part of the process will allow you to stay focused on the end goal.

Thus, creating good habits in the early phase is crucial to success. Your habits play a huge role in staying focused. One habit that many successful people have is planning your day. But before you start planning your day, plan your week. A relaxed Sunday afternoon is a good time to plan your strategy for what you want to accomplish for the week. This allows you to set some key goals for the week and will give you a framework for daily activities. In this way, you have already established the outlook for the week, so your daily goals will flow more efficiently, and you will see the best results.

This is the same as writing what you want to achieve this month, this year, next, etc. If you have inspiring goals in place, this will help you stay focused on both short-term actions and long-term outlook. Doing this every day will help you stay fully focused on doing what you need to do to be successful.

At times, there will be no one to tell you what to do and provide you with a vision or the resources to achieve your goals. It is for this reason that you are solely responsible for your success, which is why you must create a system of good habits to stay focused.

Also, you should be able to adapt to your environment and do what it takes to make yourself successful. This concept and staying focused may seem contradictory c, but they are actually complementary. Successful people agree that companies rarely go as planned. If you have a plan for what your business should look like and you are not willing to change your strategy, chances are you are not going to be successful in the long run.

If something does not work, you don't need to bang your head against the wall, trying to make it work. Instead, you must be willing to be flexible and adapt to your strategy. Being able to maintain both towards a goal is crucial to your success. Remember, sometimes, the journey will take you on multiple routes.

As I have gained experience in my career so far, I can tell you that success is a journey to travel with others. No matter what business you are in, you need to win people and develop your professional and social network. This way, you can have people always around to get help and advice. Asking for help is always a wise step, but ensure that your source of help is reliable.

Has it happened to you that you feel you're in a vicious circle when faced with a problem, and you cannot find the solution? The first thing we must understand is that we cannot always solve everything by ourselves and that it is valid to ask for help when we are faced with a situation beyond our control. One of the options is to go to coaching as a tool to grow together and expand our limits. In this book, I have tried my best to enlighten you with my personally tested and effective advice.

It could be said that since time immemorial, humanity has evolved from the exercise of coaching, though it was not called that at that time. In ancient Greece, Socrates, the philosopher, developed a method through which he promoted the process of questions and answers to reach knowledge. He started from the principle that every person has the potential within them to get the answers to their questions since wisdom resides in each one of us, and we simply must ask ourselves the appropriate questions to reach enlightenment. Socrates named it as a maieutic, which in Greek means midwife, in order to convey that the teacher was an assistant to give birth to knowledge.

Unlike talking to a friend or receiving psychological therapy, coaching requires the willingness of the individual to commit and want to change their reality. Thus, it is necessary to believe that we can beat the odds, achieve our goals, or our desired situation, and grow further. If we do this accompanied by the guidance of a coach, who has the proper preparation and our confidence, success will be ours. There are times in life that deserve to show how much you love yourself, and coaching is one more tool to show us affection.

CHAPTER EIGHT

JUST THE BEGINNING

Our life is a collection of so many events; some good and some bad ones. Of course, no one likes to have bad events, but let me assure you that they are necessary too. These good and bad events actually help us create a balance in life. As I said earlier, mistakes and failures offer opportunities to learn the best lessons to steer our life on the progressive path. Ups and downs! And this is how life goes on.

Thus, I firmly believe that everything that happened in my life has happened for a reason. When I look at everything I have gone through, I know it all played a part in who and where I am today.

TAKE OFF

> *"Every event has a purpose and every setback its lesson. I have realized that failure, whether of personal, professional or even spiritual kind, is essential to personal expansion. It brings inner growth and a whole host of psychic rewards. Never regret your past. Rather, embrace it as the teacher that it is."*
> —Robin Sharma

So, everything happens for some reason in your life, and it is up to you to turn these hardships into opportunities to make things better. After many years of receiving severe blows from life due to my own decisions, I reached a point where I considered life my enemy. I just hated it, but life is a blessing, and every moment must be cherished. Take your life as it comes, finding opportunities for the better. When we try to confront it, the consequences can be lethal. You actually confront the positive version of yourself and let that negative version thrive.

There is a multitude of things that have happened to you that lead you to hate your own life. You believe that you don't deserve bad things; it may be so, but you may need those blows to bounce back and reach the top of the tree.

If you find yourself in the middle point where you think unfair things are happening to you, and you are on the verge of going to the dark side, you must not quit yet. I encourage you to avoid the same mistakes I made in my life; as you have read in previous chapters, the consequences were devastating. Here, I want you to believe that everything happens for a reason, and that is how I live my life.

Here, I want to identify the reasons why bad things can happen to you. One reason, I believe, is ignorance, which is a lack of knowledge and/or experience.

If you don't know what fire is, you won't know that if you get too close to it, you will burn yourself, and this will cause pain.

Yes, it seems very obvious, and it is. When you get burned, you learn that you should not touch the fire, and you never do it again.

The problem comes when we ignore a multitude of details that are not so obvious, and we keep "burning" day after day without realizing it.

In my case, I kept burning myself with my not-so-good habits. We must stop ignoring details that can lead us to catastrophic consequences throughout our lives.

In your path to stop your sufferings, you need to realize and follow by correct thinking, action, care, and focus.

TAKE OFF

To make it easier, I will give an example:

Suppose you are in love with your partner. On the other hand, you are easily and often attracted to other people. Here, you have not become unfaithful, but your thoughts are so frequent that they generate an unsatisfied need that becomes greater; this causes you to be indecisive, and as a consequence, you suffer.

Without realization, your mind has been feeding a thought that has caused you suffering, and you are completely ignoring that this thought is the cause of your suffering. Thus, we all make many mistakes day after day as a result of ignorance.

When we leave ignorance behind, we stop making mistakes that cause suffering. Sometimes, these mistakes become invisible to us if we don't do our part to realize and see them. Not everything is as perceptible as knowing that you should not touch the fire.

If you notice, you can see that monks and wise people are happy, even if they have nothing. And then you can see people with thick piles of money, but they possess such a complex and ignorant mind that they can't avoid going through sufferings.

The other reason is doing the wrong thing without being ignorant.

You know that fire burns. Would you still put your hand? The obvious answer would be NO.

Oddly enough, every day, we make mistakes that we are aware of. We know what we shouldn't, yet we end up doing them since we are weak at times. For example, people who smoke know that tobacco kills, but they still smoke. Therefore, we must not only focus on not ignoring the mistakes but also stop making the mistakes that we just don't ignore. If we don't, the consequences of life will manifest sooner or later.

When life punishes us, two things can happen. Firstly, we rebel against life and sink even further as I did. Secondly, we learn from our mistakes and that we need to do. I can guarantee you that there is no better thing than trying to learn from your mistakes. I am fully convinced that if you decide to take the blows of life in a constructive way, things will be much better for you. For me, they did.

"If you're going through hell, keep going."
—*Winston Churchill*

TAKE OFF

The bumps of life simply tell us that we are not doing the right thing. When I decided to stop fighting life and made it my teacher, things started to go much better for me, and little by little, I have been coming out of the pit I pushed myself into.

The whole time I spent in that dark pit, I had the strength within me to come out.

Now, every time something happens to me, I try to get to the source and see why it happened to me. There are things that are very obvious, but others are not so obvious, and sometimes, it can be difficult to find answers. Anyway, you must never give up; keep trusting in life and that everything happens for a reason.

There are very deep aspects of our being, the result of our experiences that make us ignore small details, that little by little become bigger and cause us suffering. I understand that leaving ignorance behind is neither an easy nor a quick process. You can come out on top with your realization, will, and strength. In the end, it will be a question of your belief and being willing to do things correctly.

> *"The only thing that's the end of the world is the end of the world."*
> —*Barack Obama*

Where I'm today, I'm happy and grateful. I'm sober, seriously, this time for life. I can be that father to Jackson who I should have been since I heard the news of his conception. Now, I'm sure that I can live a calm life and be there for those who matter the most to me.

I am grateful to God and other people in my life for helping me regain my life and business. My businesses are starting to take off. I'm focused on my work. It's amazing to look back at where I thought I would never get back on my feet. When I help others, I usually get guys saying, "Nick, how did you do it?" I can only share my experience of what worked for me, but they have to do the work. I took ACTION, which is such a tough thing to do when everything in your life is spiralling, and you are going downhill.

It doesn't matter where you are with your life, whether you are thirty-four years old like me, sixty, or nineteen, whatever you CAN, change, and don't let anyone stop you from doing so.

I get pitched a lot of business opportunities and always have over the years. Most people fear failure, and it's stopping them from doing what they want to do, and they ask me for advice. I give them the best advice I can. I have a huge network with many entrepreneurs and business owners, and I pick their brains on things, and I learn every day.

Everyone has a story and worked to get where they are; it's not a perfect road. When I first started going to meetings, I had an older friend who gave me a rock that said "Faith" on it. I kept that rock in my pocket, and it helped me over my first two years of sobriety. Then passed it on to a young gentleman who's in early recovery.

THE NICK DAVIS GROUP

The Nick Davis Group is my real estate company. We are growing rapidly, and I'm happy with the progress. My sales are going up, and I hope to take the brand to the next level. I have a great team that works together, and we understand each other. I'm building a culture. Life is too short not to be happy; I make sure anyone that is and potentially could be part of the team is a perfect fit. I've had a vision for my real estate team for a long time, and now that I'm executing it with absolute focus, I think the sky is the limit.

NICK DAVIS

NICK DAVIS COACHING & RECOVERY

Over the past three years, I've had so many people say, "Nick, you need to share your story. It would help if you let people know that there's hope to those who are struggling; you need people to see your success and recovery story."

Although I thought carefully about being open publicly regarding my sobriety, I feel like, in today's day and age, we need to help each other. Life is a game, and it can throw you roadblocks. To look at doing this, I finished a Life Coaching certificate and a diploma in Drug & Alcohol Treatment from Stratford Career Institute.

I have put together a program that helps people who are struggling with addiction and in life. I want to motivate people. The death rate from addiction and mental health makes me sick, but this is the bitter reality. In all seriousness, I took things for granted and abused my body with alcohol. I don't know how I survived as long as I did. Everyone deserves a second chance, and I want to help those who are struggling. I have a passion for helping people.

It's amazing to think that life is ahead of me now. It's not all roses and rainbows, as a friend of mine, Steve says. I have some shitty days, I have some good days, but I don't have to go back to being the old Nick. I can be a new Nick

TAKE OFF

who wants to help and be there for my son. I'm not perfect, and I do still make mistakes, but at least when I do, I can quickly make my amends and try to correct them. I have a great sponsor, Scott, who has helped me clean up my wreckage from the past over the years. He's someone I can call when things aren't going my way, and I get a little fired up about something. Scott has seen me get sober and change my life around, and we enjoy golf during the summers and have a great relationship. He is a businessman himself, I can talk to him about my business and pick his brain a little bit; not only that but Scott has been in my shoes, so he gets it.

Before I finish this book, I would like to thank you for taking the time out for reading my book. I hope it will help you build your life and business and always be brave enough to beat the odds.

As we have reached almost the end of this book, I would like to tell you that I have found a special one in my life — Kathleen — the woman I can't imagine my life without.

We all, at one point or another, meet a special person. And almost all of us make the same mistake — let them slip away. Let me tell you that you must never make the mistake of losing all the special people in your life.

The worst thing is that, almost always, we realize their importance when it is too late. That is, when they have already left or when there is no longer any possibility of them coming back.

I believe that a special person in your life is the one who brings out the best in you, wants the best for you, makes you feel good and comfortable about yourself, allows you to be you, understands you, listens to you, and is always there for you. A special person appears at the right time and in the right place to help you fulfill your purpose and continue to grow.

Thus, a special person can be your partner, a friend, parents, siblings, kids, mentors, someone who changed the way you see life, or someone who appeared as if by magic when things got ugly.

Luckily, I have had so many special people in my life. Just like we usually do with health and money, we tend not to value those special people until we lose them. And unluckily, I also once distanced from them.

Generally speaking, we are unappreciative when we have everything we need and tend to think that this is normal, but it is never like that.

TAKE OFF

At any moment, we can lose everything, and things can change forever. In fact, life is unpredictable where nothing remains forever, and that includes bad times too.

Most of the time, we end up taking special people in our life for granted. Ultimately, we assume that they are always going to be there, no matter what happens. And this is where problems begin since we stop valuing and giving the attention they deserve. Just like ourselves, they need to continually be addressed, valued, and loved. Unfortunately, we don't always realize it and let them slip away.

Special people come into your life at the right time and place, and sometimes when you least expect them to appear. Therefore, when one comes into your life, you must be able to identify them.

When I found Kathleen, we didn't have a great start. In fact, she outrightly refused to even start a relationship.

After getting out of a relationship in December 2019, I took some time to focus on myself and which direction I wanted to go, taking time to continue to focus on being a father to Jackson, my business, and self-care. After all, I need to look good in my suits, right? I decided to start dating again.

I started talking to a beautiful lady named Kathleen Black online. She claimed I added her on social media. I joked around and said she added me. We were chatting here and there, but she wasn't giving me much attention. She eventually started too, and it led to long and meaningful phone calls. She mentioned she was looking for a life partner, the real thing; I could tell it in her voice. She sparked my interest high but said she doesn't date anyone in the business as she runs her own real estate coaching company.

I was very interested in meeting Kathleen, and she agreed to go to dinner with me. But wait? For some reason, I decided not to speak to her for three days before we were supposed to go. Kathleen wasn't impressed and cancelled our first date. I remember how pissed I was as I actually was looking forward to it.

We then eventually started talking again, and she agreed to meet me; I guess I had one last shot. With her living far from where I am, we decided to meet in downtown Toronto as it was somewhat of a neutral location. It was a summer July evening, and I remember her pulling up to meet me with that beautiful bright smile. I got out and hugged her, and kissed her on the cheek.

TAKE OFF

She ran a little late, which didn't bother me because I was that excited to meet her. You see, there was something different about Kathleen, something I felt the moment she came into my car to head to a nice Italian restaurant patio. We sat there for hours chatting and enjoyed a nice meal getting to know each other. I shared with her my story; you see, honesty is important in everything. We had a great conversation as I got to know a lot about her, and she got to know a lot about me. Looking into her eyes, I knew we had something.

We finished the meal and went for a drive up and down Yonge Street downtown. We were driving south towards the harbour; we kept hitting red lights, and every red light I hit, I wanted to kiss her; I eventually did. To finish the evening, we went for a walk by the harbour and talked for hours. Ever since that evening, we have been inseparable.

Kathleen understands me, and I understand her; I care and love her. I think God put her in my life, and I'm truly grateful for that. To describe Kathleen in a nutshell, she's everything I have ever imagined my life partner to be. Caring, loving, honest, faithful, trustworthy, beautiful, smart, and consistent. She's real and understands me. We have a future together, and be prepared to see my new book out next year!

Everything in life can change with the blink of an eye. A great friend can stop being a great friend at any moment. Similarly, your love can end when you least imagine it. People, just as they arrive at the right time, also leave at the right time so that they can follow their path and allow you to continue yours. However, everything those special people bring you is something you will only experience in the same way with them, and with no one others.

Thus, when you are together, take care of them, value them, and make the most of every moment you share.

Enjoy every conversation with your mother, father, siblings, children, and friends, and share every achievement with them. Savor the joy of every hug you receive and every moment of laughter or tears you live with them.

And, when necessary, let go and allow yourself to be free to start over from scratch with other people. Sometimes, life leads us to farewells and separations that we have to face to continue growing. However, never let them slip away because you don't know how to appreciate and value them as they deserve. Never lose them, thinking that you will find other ones whenever you want or need them. And never miss an opportunity, a conversation, or a good deed, thinking that you can get it back at another time.

TAKE OFF

That day may never come. I can assure you that someone special in your life is a rare treasure.

Once again, thank you for taking the time to read my journey, and remember, NEVER QUIT!

ACKNOWLEDGEMENT

I'd like to thank Mom, Dad, Cheryl, Diana, Alan, Debra and family, Linsey Fisher with the help of the direction of the book and title, Scott C, The Cutlers, Uncle Mike and family, Andrew, S.C., K.C., J.S., C.R., S.S., G.M., S.D., M.B., P.D., S.D., V.S., V.C., C.M., J.T., R.L., B.M., R.B., T.M., J.M., Kathleen and everyone who encouraged me to share my story and has helped me over the years; you know who you are, and I'll be forever grateful for that.

ABOUT THE AUTHOR

NICK DAVIS is a Canadian entrepreneur based out of Oakville, Ontario Canada, a real estate broker specializing in the Oakville, Burlington, and the GTA West area luxury market, and an author and life coach focusing on self-development and helping people recover from addiction.

NICK DAVIS INC.
www.nickdavisinc.com

NICK DAVIS GROUP
www.thenickdavisgroup.com

www.nickdaviscoaching.com

Made in the USA
Monee, IL
25 January 2021